The Monetarist Counter-Revolution

A Critique of Canadian Monetary Policy 1975-1979

The **Canadian Institute for Economic Policy** has been established to engage in public discussion of fiscal, industrial and other related public policies designed to strengthen Canada in a rapidly changing international environment.

The Institute will fulfill this mandate by sponsoring and undertaking studies pertaining to the economy of Canada and disseminating such studies. Its intention is to contribute in an innovative way to the development of public policy in Canada.

The Monetarist Counter-Revolution

A Critique of Canadian Monetary Policy 1975-1979

Arthur W. Donner and Douglas D. Peters

James Lorimer & Company, Publishers
in association with the
Canadian Institute for Economic Policy
Toronto 1979

The opinions expressed in this study are those of the authors alone and are not intended to represent those of any organization with which they may be associated.

ISBN 0-88862-272-4 cloth
ISBN 0-88862-273-2 paper

6 5 4 3 2 1   79 80 81 82 83 84 85

Canadian Cataloguing in Publication Data
  Donner, Arthur W., 1937–
    The monetarist counter-revolution

  ISBN 0-88862-272-4 bd. ISBN 0-88862-273-2 pa.

  1. Monetary policy – Canada. 2. Canada – Economic
  policy – 1971–   * I. Peters, Douglas D., 1930–
  II. Title.

  HC115.D652   339.5′3′0971   C79-094662-9

Additional copies of this book
may be purchased from:

James Lorimer & Company, Publishers
Egerton Ryerson Memorial Building
35 Britain Street,
Toronto M5A 1R7, Ontario

Printed and bound in Canada

Contents

Tables and Charts

Foreword

In publishing this study by Dr. Donner and Dr. Peters, the Canadian Institute for Economic Policy is fulfilling its wish to contribute to public discussion of the appropriateness of monetary policy in recent years.

The authors argue that monetarism failed in Canada in the post-1975 period because it did not lend itself to dealing with the structural aspects of inflation and because, along with other policies, it did not alleviate the growing balance of payments deficit.

The authors believe that Canada must adopt a strategy for balancing the current account in the medium term. They also propose the implementation of a tax-based incomes policy as one means of dealing with inflation and unemployment problems. In addition, they advocate important changes in the mode of policy formulation by the Bank of Canada in order to increase the openness and visibility of its deliberative processes.

These and other recommendations will, the Institute hopes form a basis for vigorous public debate. The analysis and conclusions are however those of the authors and do not necessarily reflect the views of the Institute.

J. J. Shepherd
President

Canadian Institute for Economic Policy

Acknowledgements

The authors are pleased to acknowledge the considerable efforts of others who have aided in the completion of this manuscript. But while we accepted help from many individuals, we retain the rights to all the errors that may be found; nor do we wish in any way to imply that those named below necessarily agree with our conclusions.

The Canadian Institute for Economic Policy offered encouragement and valuable criticism in the preparation of this study. We are especially indebted to Professor Abraham Rotstein and the Honourable Walter Gordon for their considerable efforts. The referees contributed important ideas for which we are grateful. Professor Clarence Barber, Dr. Donner's economics teacher at the University of Manitoba, once more has offered direct and pertinent comments. As former University of Pennsylvania students, we would also like to mention our intellectual debts to Professors Sidney Weintraub and Charles R. Whittlesey.

Our editor, Diane Nelles, added greatly to the readability and clarity of the text, and we are pleased to acknowledge her help. Mrs. Mary Dagonas typed the manuscript and wrestled with our hieroglyphics.

We also recognize the contribution of our wives, Gail and Audrey. Having listened to us argue with each other for over fifteen years, they were convinced that we would be unable to agree on anything let alone complete this study. They were also delighted when we proved them wrong.

The Background to the Adoption of Monetarism

This book is concerned with the important change that took place in Canada's monetary policy in 1975. We are, of course, aware that one facet of economic policy should not be considered in isolation from the influence of other policies and events. But while we recognize that many policies shaped economic events in the 1970s, we nevertheless decided to limit the major orientation of this study to monetary policy.

Responsibility for monetary policy rests with the Bank of Canada, which is charged

> to regulate credit and currency in the best interests of the economic life of the nation, to control and protect the external value of the national monetary unit and to mitigate by its influence fluctuations in the general level of production, trade, prices and employment, so far as may be possible within the scope of monetary action, and generally to promote the economic and financial welfare of the Dominion.[1]

The Bank operates on a day-to-day basis as an independent entity, but political control is maintained through the consultation that is required between the Governor of the Bank of Canada and the Minister of Finance. In the event of a difference of opinion the Minister has the responsibility in conjunction with the Cabinet to "give to the Governor a written directive concerning monetary policy, in specific terms and applicable for a specified period and the Bank shall comply with such directive."[2] This ensures that the final responsibility for monetary policy rests with the Minister of Finance, the Cabinet, and the federal government. A further result is the integration of government economic policies with monetary policy.

This study was prompted by our feeling that something went wrong with Canada's economy in the late 1970s when all seemingly reasonable policy goals suddenly became unattainable despite the initiation of a plethora of programmes to help attain these elusive economic objectives. The Bank's new policy for attaining the objectives of monetary policy was labelled "monetarism."

In this chapter we examine the factors that led to the adoption of the new monetary policy goals in 1975. A review of the theory and practice of monetarism is presented in Chapter 2. The third chapter considers how this new doctrine was interpreted and applied in Canada. The important new problem of structural inflation that emerged in the 1970s is discussed in Chapter 4. Chapters 5 and 6 change the focus from the late 1970s to the 1980s and review domestic and international concerns for the future. There is a summing up in the final Chapter 7. The study considers two additional specific technical issues: the problems of setting and achieving money supply targets in Appendix A; and the issue of disclosure of information on the formulation of monetary policy in Appendix B.

The Scene in the Early 1970s

Inflation in the western world accelerated in the mid-1970s following a series of crop failures in 1972 and the fourfold increase in oil prices in 1973. In the early 1970s the monetary stance in most industrial nations was expansive, reflecting more concern with economic growth than inflation. As a result of the wave of inflation, however, central banks generally became sensitive to the charge that they were fuelling inflation, and priorities began to shift in the world monetary and fiscal power centres towards curtailing inflationary pressures.

The Bank of Canada as the monetary authority in this country had similarly been attacked by many influential economists who argued that its performance was largely responsible for the rising rate of inflation between 1970 and 1975. While not explicitly accepting all of their criticisms, the Bank responded to their complaints in 1975 by adopting a policy of deliberately but gradually slowing the growth rate in the money supply following a game plan that had been introduced several years earlier in the United States.

But was central bank policy in Canada so unsuccessful in the early 1970s that a change was necessary? And did that change remedy the inflation problem? The expansionary policies of the early decade had promoted economic growth, but they also led to serious inflation that had to be dealt with. The solution, however, did not result in a lower inflation rate and, because of more restrictive macroeconomic policies, Canada's economic growth rate was significantly slower than that achieved in the previous decade. Before examining the effects of monetarist policy in Canada during the latter half of the seventies, it is interesting to note several other factors that were conducive to the adoption of such a new stance.

Bank of Canada Policies, 1970-74

As the Canadian economy recovered from the 1970 recession, the Bank of Canada was primarily concerned with two issues: the desire to maintain relatively easy credit conditions and at the same time to prevent undue appreciation of the external value of the Canadian dollar. Both objectives were consistent with the need for strong economic recovery in Canada. Essentially the Bank recognized that the expansion of the economy required that the international current account be in relative balance so that inflows of capital would not force that account sharply into deficit and restrict domestic economic growth.[3]

Though the economy continued to expand throughout 1972, the Bank was dissatisfied with economic performance, which "was less satisfactory than had been hoped for ... as unemployment remained high and prices rose more rapidly than in the previous year."[4] At the same time, the Bank also recognized that structural changes in the economy had raised the unemployment rate and that "although there is undoubtedly too much slack in the economy, there is ... some reason to believe that unemployment rates may no longer reflect the same degree of ease in the labour market as they formerly did."[5] The Bank acknowledged as well the interrelation of the current and capital account and admitted that it was mainly in trying to achieve "a balance on capital account appropriate to the balance on current account, that Canada has had a problem in recent years."[6] The Bank was concerned about undue appreciation of the exchange rate that would result from a large inflow of capital, and the Governor specifically supported the Minister of Finance's guidelines for Canadian borrowers, urging them to search aggressively for funds in Canada before issuing securities abroad. The Bank's 1972 Report also expressed concern over rising inflation and wage rates.

By 1973 economic circumstances had changed, and the Bank soon altered the relatively easy credit conditions that prevailed until the beginning of the year. The move to restraint was caused by "an upwards spiral of price increases for farm and industrial commodities of an intensity without modern precedent."[7]

But rapid expansion of the Canadian economy in 1973 also included some positive effects. Just prior to the sharp rise in world oil prices, Canada witnessed marked increases in the prices of many of its commodity exports in international markets. In particular, both mineral and agricultural prices rose rapidly in 1973. Raw materials exports produced high returns and prices for manufactured imports continued to remain relatively low. The result was that Canada's terms of trade improved by some 6 per cent, the current account deficit declined to only $330 million,[8] and new issues of bonds to non-residents fell off markedly.[9]

Canada is, and was at that time, a net exporter of energy.[10] Thus, when energy prices, particularly crude oil prices, rose dramatically in 1973, Canada was in an extremely enviable position as the only major industrial nation self-sufficient in energy. Other industrial nations saw the OPEC price increase as a massive negative change in their terms of trade. For Canada, the reverse was true. The rise in energy prices in themselves generated a small positive change in the terms of trade.

The substantial improvement in Canada's terms of trade created both an opportunity and a particular problem for policymakers. Clearly the magnitude of the price hikes for industrial and food exports surprised the Bank. But the authorities should also have recognized that this improvement in the terms of trade was transitory and would be quickly reflected in increased prices for the manufactured goods purchased abroad. This sharp improvement in the terms of trade presented the Bank with two options: either accommodate domestic inflation, or allow the external value of the Canadian dollar to appreciate. The authorities chose the inflation route.

Both of these choices were, of course, detrimental to the development of Canadian industry and particularly the manufacturing sector. Canada had experienced difficulty in developing this sector over the years and the deficit in international trade in manufactured goods continued to enlarge in the early 1970s. The improvement in the terms of trade, because of the rapidly increasing prices of primary goods exports, quickly translated into rapidly rising domestic costs. This secondary effect placed further pressure on the manufacturing sector and led to a relative decline that only began to reverse in the late 1970s following the significant depreciation of the external value of the Canadian dollar. Had policymakers decided to allow the exchange rate to appreciate in 1973, the effect would likely have been equally destructive to Canada's manufacturing industries. An exchange rate appreciation would have made Canadian manufactured goods more expensive in world markets and foreign goods less expensive in Canada. Both

4

CHART 1-1

INDEX OF TERMS OF TRADE, CANADA, 1969-78

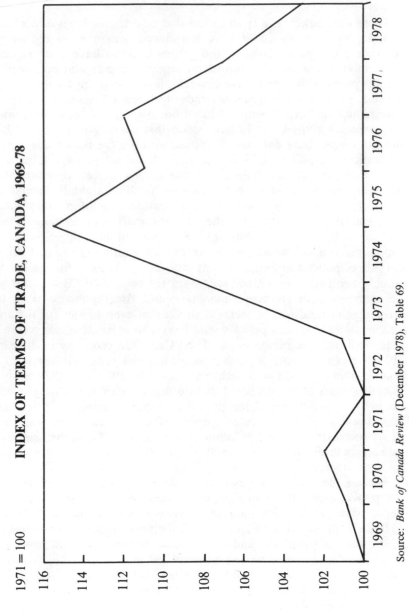

1971 = 100

Source: *Bank of Canada Review* (December 1978), Table 69.

effects would have retarded the domestic output of manufactured products.

There was, however, a third choice that could have been undertaken at that time. Ottawa could have introduced measures to reduce resource exports, particularly oil and gas, or it could have encouraged a substantial current account surplus by repaying the capital borrowed in earlier years. This latter choice would have been in Canada's best interest, for when the terms of trade declined in ensuing years, the current account surpluses and reduced borrowing, and thus lower interest payments abroad, would have stood this country in good stead. A policy to repurchase debt issues abroad would have required a tighter domestic fiscal policy in 1973 and would have produced a substantial budget surplus for the federal government. A more accommodative monetary policy could have been followed that might have allowed relatively lower interest rates. Such a combination of policies would have encouraged borrowing in the domestic market rather than abroad and would have given government the surplus funds to move out of the capital markets in Canada and make room for others. In sum, a different mix of policies at that turbulent time in Canada's economic history would have better served our long-term interests. In 1973 the authorities pursued both restrictive monetary and fiscal policies. With the advantage of hindsight, it seems clear that an even tighter fiscal stance and an easier monetary policy would have had more desirable results.

In retrospect the performance of the Canadian economy in the early 1970s was vastly superior to that in subsequent years. Higher rates of real economic growth were achieved between 1970 and 1974 than in the latter years of the decade. Inflation was high in 1974, the year that marked the beginning of the period of rapid inflation in prices and costs because of the structural impact of energy and high wage and salary increases. The high inflation of 1973 and 1974 and the associated rapid growth in the money supply set the stage for the abrupt change to monetarism in 1975.

At the same time a combination of factors led Canadian officials and the public generally to become complacent about Canada's international payments position—a complacency that vanished in 1977 and 1978. In 1975 the Bank of Canada and the federal government chose to ignore the exchange rate and the balance of payments and instead to embark upon a new direction dictated by monetarists' objectives. In addition, the high exchange rates that resulted from the tight monetary policies pursued in 1974 and 1976 caused a major slowdown in the real growth of the Canadian economy.

6

Political Aspects of the Shift to Monetarism

Any major shift in economic policy can be made significantly easier if the political climate is favourable to the change. For example, in the late 1940s and 1950s there was a preoccupation with avoiding depression conditions and consequently the public was prepared for vigorous fiscal initiatives. In the case of the shift to monetarism in the 1970s, several political aspects made the change generally acceptable and encouraged its development.

The 1970s saw the emergence of a major rightward shift in the mainstream of political and economic thought not only in Canada but in many industrial countries in the western world. In part, this phenomenon was a response to the problem of rising inflation and the belief that social welfare programs had proceeded too far too rapidly and contributed to that inflation.

Inflation rates in the major industrial countries had assumed what

TABLE 1-1
ANNUAL RATE OF CHANGE IN CONSUMER PRICE INDEXES
IN SELECTED OECD COUNTRIES, 1963-75

	Average 1963-71	1973	1974	1975
Canada	3.3	7.6	10.9	10.8
United States	3.5	6.2	11.0	9.1
Japan	5.5	11.7	23.2	11.7
Australia	3.5	9.4	15.1	15.1
New Zealand		8.2	11.1	14.7
Austria	3.7	7.5	9.5	8.5
Belgium	3.7	7.0	12.7	12.7
Denmark	6.1	9.3	15.0	11.0
Finland	5.6	10.5	17.5	17.6
France	4.2	7.3	13.7	11.7
Germany	3.0	6.9	7.0	6.0
Italy	3.7	10.4	19.4	17.2
Netherlands	5.4	8.0	9.7	10.2
Norway	5.1	7.0	9.8	11.9
Sweden	4.8	6.1	13.8	9.2
Switzerland	3.8	8.7	9.8	6.7
United Kingdom	5.0	8.3	16.0	24.1

Source: OECD, *Main Economic Indicators* (December 1972; October 1976).

were widely perceived to be crisis proportions (Table 1-1). This was one effect of the adjustment to the rapid rise in mineral and agricultural prices and the compounding of those price increases by the oil price hikes of 1973 and 1974. In Canada the trend to higher inflation was shown by the broadest inflation measure, the implicit price deflator, which rose 9.1 per cent in 1973 and 15.3 per cent in 1974, compared with a maximum rate of only 5 per cent in the previous twenty-one years and an average rate of 2.5 per cent between 1952 and 1972. In the United States, higher rates of inflation were also experienced when the implicit price deflator rose 9.7 per cent in 1974 and 9.6 per cent in 1975.

When there are different rates of inflation among the various commodities and service groups, the effects on incomes vary widely; that is, shifts in relative prices result in shifts in the distribution of income. This can result in more social dissension as one income group may see pronounced windfall gains in others' rising incomes. This compounded the political difficulties of income inequalities.

In addition, during the 1973-75 period alarm was expressed at the rising share of government activity in total gross national expenditure. Part of this concern emanated from those on the political right who began to argue that social welfare spending, which had increased rapidly in most countries, was both extravagant and unproductive. There was, indeed, mounting evidence, particularly in North America, that many of the social programmes had not only failed to achieve their objectives but had also been vastly more expensive than was originally anticipated. In Canada growing attention was directed towards statements showing how the government share of GNP had risen significantly in the postwar years.

Monetary policy had also received some very negative reviews in the early 1970s in the press and among academics.[11] It was viewed as a cause or a least a contributor to the very rapid rate of inflation that occurred in most countries in the mid-1970s. Monetary policy was also viewed as the handmaiden of large government deficits—which had allowed governments to continue the very rapid increases in spending that had occurred.[12] Thus by the mid-1970s Canadian monetary authorities were on the defensive and indeed had accepted much of the unfavourable criticism directed at their policies. This was a sharp change from the past, when the reputation of the monetary authority was regarded as almost beyond reproach.[13]

Along with this more negative view of the policies of the Bank of Canada emerged what seemed to be a shift in political power and

8

economic influence away from that institution to others in Ottawa. To outsiders it appeared that the Department of Finance had gathered to itself a number of experts in monetary policy when its role had traditionally been limited to fiscal policy. Joining the Department of Finance in the late 1960s and early 1970s were three of Canada's leading experts in money and banking, each of whom had impressive credentials in the monetary area. Each had been a professor of money and banking at a major Canadian university and each had written extensively on money and banking topics including articles and books accepted as scholarly works. The Department was also headed by a politically influential deputy minister. This gathering of monetary talent gave the Department of Finance intimidating new expertise in monetary policy when, in the past, it had left monetary details to the Bank. An even more important shift in power and influence was underway in Ottawa at this time to the office of the Prime Minister and of the Privy Council, where economic advisers appeared to become the chief instigators of new policies and of analyses of existing programmes.

This apparent diminution in power and influence of the Bank, combined with a public belief in its fallibility, made the shift to monetarist doctrines both possible and palatable. The monetarist doctrine gave the Bank clear and precise goals that could be easily assessed by the general public and by the now more powerful Department of Finance and offices of the Prime Minister and Privy Council. The Bank could now point to its goals and was more clearly accountable for their achievement.

Conclusion
In the first half of the 1970s, the Bank of Canada suddenly faced a new type of structural inflation. The Bank was also subject to mounting criticism of its earlier expansionary policies, which were blamed for the rising rate of inflation in 1973 and 1974. As inflation rose, the political environment became more conservative in tone, and the public tended to be more concerned with monetary policy matters. In these circumstances the Bank of Canada announced its conversion to the monetarist principles of slowing the growth rate in the money supply over the longer term. In fact, monetary policy subsequently contributed to a worsening economic performance and a disastrous international payments position without having much impact on inflation. The theoretical framework supporting the growing acceptance of monetarist central bank principles is considered in the following chapter.

Interpreting the Monetarist Doctrine

The criticism that the Bank of Canada's policies contributed to inflation in the early 1970s must be considered in the context of a continuing theoretical debate about the proper role of the monetary authority. Indeed, since the publication of Keynes' General Theory in 1935, there has been an ongoing debate among academic and practising economists about money and its role in the process of economic growth and inflation. With the general acceleration of inflation since the early 1960s, the debate reheated and the labels applied to the major protagonists changed slightly.[1]

The key participants in the recent debate are divided loosely into two groups known as post-Keynesians and monetarists. In the United States the former are represented by economists such as Lawrence Klein, Paul Samuelson, James Tobin, and Sidney Weintraub. These so-called post-Keynesians support the tradition of economic intervention in an economy that is inherently unable to achieve a non-inflationary full-employment equilibrium. On the other side of the debate is the group of economists described as monetarists who believe the key to economic stability is stable growth in the money supply. Their most prominent spokesman is Milton Friedman. In Canada, monetarism was vigorously promoted by Tom Courchene of the University of Western Ontario and George Freeman of the Bank of Canada.[2]

Courchene's work is important to acknowledge, for not only is he an articulate spokesman for the monetarist position, he also systematically reviewed Bank of Canada policy and set himself up as a one-man watchdog to ensure that the Bank of Canada remained faithful to its monetarist commitments. His conclusion is that, according to orthodox monetarism, the Bank has fulfilled at least part of its necessary new mandate.

In Courchene's view, the same type of shift the U.S. Federal Reserve

System made from monitoring
money supply growth rates is
Canada. Implied is acceptance o
ment that inflation is always and e
indeed, Courchene even draws att
ogy of the Bank's pronouncements a
Friedman. Courchene considers that "
Canada probably qualifies for the d
monetarist central bank."[3] In fact, pur
quarrel with the monetarist labelling of p
policy, since the Bank intervened heavily i
ket between 1977 and 1979, an action that
fluctuating currencies. In this connection C
change rates must be left free to fluctuate indep

> For a small, open economy, such as characteriz
> prescribe a monetary rule if the exchange rate is
> must be geared to balance-of-payments consideratio
> change rate (assuming, of course, that the country w
> pegged value of the exchange rate), and this preclud
> monetary policy, such as would be the case if Canada ac
> rule.[4]

As a guideline for evaluating Canada's monetarist
Courchene's studies provide unequivocal support for win
money supply growth rates and abandoning interest rates a
for Canadian policy. The Courchene approach is, however, hig
cal of the recent exchange rate intervention exercises in Cana
large government deficits.[5]

While Courchene's views represent monetarists' position
clearly, it is still difficult to separate concisely that school of thou
from that of the post-Keynesians. Several points are, however, oft
accented in any discussions of their analytical differences.

- To the monetarist the growth trend in the money supply is a
  dominant determinant of the price level whether or not the economy is at full capacity and full employment. The post-Keynesian
  would expect monetary policy to affect output and employment
  and, through them indirectly, the price level. In the long run both
  groups would agree that, in theory, stable prices require growth in
  the money supply equal to growth in full-capacity output.

...onetarists contend that fiscal actions designed to expand an ...ny and lower the level of unemployment can only have a ...ory and small effect. Indeed, monetarists argue that fiscal ...y can only stimulate an economy if there is an accompanying ...etary response. The post-Keynesians accept a contra-cyclical ... for fiscal policy in the economy and contend that monetary ...sures are capable of complementing or offsetting such fiscal ...sures depending upon the objectives being pursued.

...e theoretical linkage in the monetarist framework flows directly ...om money supply growth to expenditure decisions. Monetarists ...aim that the post-Keynesian view of the process—that is, that monetary policy operates primarily through interest rates on investment decisions—is incorrect.

Ideology or value judgments usually play a complementary role to economic theory in this recent debate between post-Keynesians and monetarists. A conservative ideology that tends to stress free markets and "the invisible hand" is naturally attracted to the monetarist theory, since it appears to be less interventionist and holds out greater hope for curtailing inflation. The use of fiscal policy in the post-Keynesian programme implies intervention that holds attractions for more ideologically liberal economists.[6]

- Conventional wisdom holds that post-Keynesians will accept more inflation than monetarists and, when anti-inflation measures are to be introduced, post-Keynesians tend to favour less active use of tight monetary policies in favour of some direct form of wage and price intervention.

- The debate on "does money matter" has shifted significantly from the 1950s to the 1970s. Post-Keynesians of the 1950s stressed the inability of monetary measures to revive a severely depressed economy because of a so-called liquidity-trap constraint. Simplistically, the post-Keynesian approach resulted in a "money does not matter but fiscal policy does" syndrome. Under the monetarist creed, money is virtually all that matters, and fiscal policy is insignificant. In the 1970s money matters to both groups, though the post-Keynesians stress the effects on output of monetary changes while the monetarists continue to emphasize prices.

Indeed, the "does money matter" debate—which has often been viewed by laymen as the crux of the issue separating monetarists from non-monetarists—has become somewhat redundant to professional

12

economists, since from the perspective of economic theory there seems to have been a "growing together" among both camps on the principles of how the money supply and its attendant growth affect nominal GNP.

As Franco Modigliani noted in his presidential address to the 89th meeting of the American Economic Association on September 17, 1976:

> In reality the distinguishing feature of the monetarist school and the real issues of disagreement with nonmonetarists is not monetarism, but rather the role that should probably be assigned to stabilization policies. Nonmonetarists accept what I regard to be the fundamental practical message of the *General Theory*: that a private enterprise economy using an intangible money *needs* to be stabilized, *can be* stabilized, and therefore *should* be stabilized by appropriate monetary and fiscal policies. Monetarists by contrast take the view that there is no serious need to stabilize the economy; that even if there were a need, it could not be done, for stabilization policies would be more likely to increase than to decrease instability; and, at least some monetarists would, I believe, go so far as to hold that, even in the unlikely event that stabilization policies could on balance prove beneficial, the government should not be trusted with the necessary power.[7]

Modigliani argued that the monetarist attacks on the Keynesian policies were directed not so much at the theoretical framework but at whether or not stabilization policies were actually required. He went on to point out that early postwar U.S. economic policies were still haunted by memories of the great depression and in the 1950s were framed in response to the anxiety that aggregate demand could once again become deficient and cause massive levels of unemployment. In technical terms, there was an overconcern with the liquidity trap; that is, the inability of monetary authorities to generate sufficiently low interest rates to stimulate investment. As well, early postwar policymakers tended to stress the insensitivity of investment to monetary policy and to view the investment process as inherently volatile.

Thus in the 1950s and 1960s in both Canada and the United States, economic policy stressed the full-employment goal. The accepted model of inflation centred on the aggregate demand-pull explanation. Such policies failed to distinguish between short-run and long-run propensities to save and spend and fell back on an apparent stable trade-off relationship between inflation and unemployment (the Phillips Curve). Robert Nobay and Harry G. Johnson noted

Monetarism has in large measure preferred to concentrate its attack on Keynesianism by directing attention to the dynamic shortcomings of that approach as compared with its own framework, principally its distinction between real and nominal magnitudes, the role it assigns to price expectations, and (borrowing from permanent income theory) the distinction between responses to transitory and permanent changes. Friedman's 1967 Presidential Address is a powerful and cogent attack on Keynesianism and, in particular, is known for its challenge to the Keynesian use of the Phillips Curve for the "missing equation."[8]

The demise of these postwar economic policy prescriptions parallelled theoretical and empirical developments in the 1950s and the 1960s. There were refinements and improvements in the Keynesian concept of liquidity preference and extensions and modifications in the Phillips curve literature towards the view that in the long run a permanent trade-off between inflation and unemployment does not exist. That is, over a sufficiently long time period, an economy's unemployment rate would gravitate towards its equilibrium or normal level at which point the inflation rate would presumably stabilize at a fixed rate of change.[9] In this long-run situation, inflation is a purely monetary phenomenon. As well, econometric model-builders were demonstrating that the short-run impact on an economy, emanating from an external shock, may be different than the longer-run effect.

Friedman was a very important contributor to this revival of neoclassical economic policy. His studies on the demand for money, the permanent income hypothesis, and the theory of the trade-off relationship between inflation and unemployment all seemed to point towards the view that the economy was inherently stable but was made unstable because of unwarranted and ill-advised government intervention.

Friedman proposed neutralizing the erratic effect of monetary policy on the U.S. economy by forcing the Federal Reserve System to adopt a fixed monetary rule. In the late 1950s he proposed that the money supply should grow at a fixed annual rate, which would be roughly the rate of growth of the full-employment level of output at constant prices. "Friedman's estimate for this growth rate has varied between 3 and 5 per cent with reference to narrow and broad definitions of money (those without and with time deposits included). In the late 1960's he referred to this rule as a 5 per cent rule to distinguish it from his 2 per cent rule."[10] The central notion in the Friedman 5 per cent rule is that stabilizing the growth in money stock is preferable to discretionary monetary policy, no matter what the rate of growth of money supply. Other key ideas in the Friedman proposal are that the lags in the effects of monetary policy are so long and variable that policy cannot adequately offset or reinforce relatively unpredictable economic developments; and that positive economic benefits would accrue from the greater certainties surrounding the fixed rule, given the unpredictable and erratic variability of monetary policy.

Nobay and Johnson saw this approach as essentially a return to the pre-General Theory state of monetary economics in which the prime concern was to deal with dynamic responses to monetary disturbances.[11] Modigliani's view was different. In the closing paragraph of his presidential address, Modigliani noted: "We must, therefore, categorically reject the monetarist appeal to turn back the clock forty years by discarding the basic message of the *General Theory*. We should instead concentrate our efforts in an endeavour to make stabilization policies even more effective in the future than they have been in the past."[12]

The latest, and the most sophisticated attack on the supporters of stabilization policies was launched by a group of economists adhering to the "rational expectations theory."[13] Stated succinctly, this hypothesis assumes that information on how the economic system operates— and has changed—is quickly assimilated by the decision-makers in the economy. Thus for economic policy to have a desired impact, the participants must be surprised by government action. Any attempt to stabilize the economy by means of monetary or fiscal intervention is bound to be totally ineffective because the effects will be offset by countervailing actions adopted by those affected.

The literature and its implied attack on the role of economic stabilization measures sprung up in the 1960s when both Milton Friedman and Edmund Phelps argued that in the long run expectations of inflation must equal realized inflation and thus there could be no long-run trade-off between inflation and unemployment. The short-run, inverse relationship between inflation and unemployment only existed because some groups in society were being fooled and were underestimating the effects of inflation. This line of argument was extended into the "accelerationist" hypothesis, which concluded that in order to maintain the rate of unemployment below some natural or equilibrium level, accelerating rates of inflation would be required.

Several major problems exist with the rational expectations theory. First, the combination of the theory that focuses largely on financial markets with the vertical Phillips curve presents a too-pessimistic view of policy options. Second, the view that all unemployment in excess of the natural or equilibrium rate is transitory is clearly untenable. Third, the literature implies that the economy should respond to change swiftly, though people seem to alter their expectations only gradually. Finally, the theory fails to appreciate the costs of obtaining information and the limitations on information flows to the public.

Two sets of of empirical criticisms of the rational expectations approach are also important since they imply a role for stabilization measures. Price and wage rigidities and the existence of contracts with fixed terms dominate the short-run reality and provide a basis for effective stabilization measures. As well, the costs associated with obtaining information and the fact that information is not widely disseminated and available to all supports the use of well-understood stabilization measures.

If one were to accept the rational expectations type of world—one that had no inflexibilities and only very short-term contracts—then monetarist central bank policies should result in less inflation as long as the money supply increased at a progressively lower rate over time. Such policies would affect prices, according to this theory, primarily through their effects on capital markets. But even if market yields were assumed to adjust to inflation swiftly, as the rational expectations model would predict, it still does not mean that inflation and its impact on capital markets would be neutral for the real economy. The effects of market yields on the external value of the Canadian dollar must be considered. In addition, high inflation and the resulting high interest rates tend to retard domestic investment both because they create uncertainty over currency values and because inflation adversely affects after-tax real profits—a substantial source of investment funds.

The following sections consider the potential impact of monetarist policies on capital markets, and particularly the impact on interest rates. There are, as well, several other capital market considerations that relate more to the practice of monetary policy than to monetarism, such as the question whether government deficits crowd out private spending and how government financing through the banking system affects the capital market.

Monetarism and Market Interest Rates

Some monetarists argue that both monetary and fiscal stabilization policies in North America have, on average, been inflationary, causing wider swings in financial conditions than were necessary because of the pursuit of inappropriate goals, poor understanding of the economic system, or some combination of the two. The acceptance of monetarist principles and the pursuit of related policies would in monetarist theory have resulted in a more stable real and financial economy. Thus, in

16

theory, if central banks and national governments were able to achieve greater economic stability and lower general inflation rates via monetarist measures, *ceteris paribus*, lower interest rates would follow. Viewed from this perspective, monetarism, in theory, would result in lower interest rates and less volatile markets.

The relationship between monetary conditions, inflation, and interest rates can best be described with the aid of a simple principle articulated by Irving Fisher and subsequently extended and refined by other economists.[14] The crux of the Fisher principle is that market interest rates can be dissected into two constituent components: a real rate of return to the investor, and future expected rates of inflation over the maturity of the financial contract. If long-term government securities are currently yielding a 10 per cent annual rate of return to the investor, the 10 per cent yield would have to be discounted by the expected future rate of inflation in order to determine the real rate of return. It follows that a real rate of return could be calculated for any financial instrument if inflation expectations were known. In the above example, if the Canadian consumer price index, which rose 8 per cent in 1977, were confidently projected forward at that rate into the future, the 10 per cent government bond yield would result in a pre-tax real rate of return to the investor of 2 per cent.

Traditionally the view has been that the real return to investors is fairly stable, so that erratic changes in long-term interest rates reflect basic alterations in the inflationary climate. The Fisher principle is perfectly consistent with fundamental demand and supply explanations for interest rates. As long as the presumption is that both lenders and borrowers of funds hold identical inflationary expectations, the market rate of interest would tend to rise or fall with changes in those expectations.

As a further illustration of the relationship between inflation and interest rates generally, let us compare rates in the much less inflationary environment of the late 1960s with those a decade later. In 1967 the consumer price index rose 3.6 per cent, long-term Canadian bonds yielded an interest return of 5.9 per cent, and the prime business lending rate was 6 per cent. Inflationary expectations that year were obviously far lower than those that prevailed in 1977, when the long-term average government yield for ten-year and over securities was 8.69 per cent, the banks' prime business lending rate averaged 8.5 per cent, and the consumer price index advanced by 9.5 per cent.

Thus increases in inflation and higher expectations of future inflation generally result in higher interest rates. This principle is widely understood and accepted within the financial community. And, according to the Fisher principle, if inflation were lower and were expected to remain at such a level, this would be quickly reflected in lower long-term interest rates because of the scaling down of inflationary expectations. Few economists would quarrel with the hypothesis that lower inflation is a necessary condition for sustained lower interest rates and that if monetary policy successfully reduced the pace of inflation, lower interest rates would follow.

Monetarism and the Crowding Out Argument

A central point of contention between monetarists and non-monetarists is the so-called crowding out argument, which in turn is related to the relative strengths of monetary and fiscal measures for attaining their economic objectives. The crowding out argument is complex, as it attributes to deficit financing the crowding out of private spending that would otherwise occur.[15] The argument is also rather vague, in part because sometimes "crowding out" is defined as the unavailability of funds at any price and at other times it is described as available funds at unacceptably high interest rates.

The crowding out debate became prominent during the post-1975 period in Canada when government deficits rose dramatically from just under $1.3 billion in 1967 to an estimated $12 billion in 1978. While economists may quarrel about the best way to measure the deficit, all measures have shown particularly sharp increases since 1975. The figures used here for the budget deficit are the government of Canada's net financial requirements including foreign exchange.

Viewed in isolation from any repercussions on the growth of the economy, the greater the deficit, the higher the interest costs. To the degree that higher interest rates reflect larger government deficits, this phenomenon could result in a crowding out of private borrowing from the financial system in the sense that some interest costs may be unacceptably high in relation to prospective investor returns. Seen in this way, larger deficits deter spending in other sectors of the economy.

Stated another way, additional federal deficit financing in a fully employed economy clearly crowds out private borrowing. Thus there is a change in the composition of total GNP with a tilt in the mix in the direction of greater government than private spending and production. In an underemployed economy, however, the impact of higher federal deficit finance is less obvious. If higher deficits are largely a result of a weak economy—such as poor revenues or greater expenditures for unemployment compensation—then government sector financing may

18

be automatically compensating for weak private demand without a deliberate increase in government programmes. Indeed, there may not be any crowding out, as government could be absorbing the excess funds available because of the lowered spending intentions in the private sector.

Essentially, it is the financial system's response and reaction to deficit financing that is most important. For example, will higher deficits prompt or stimulate an additional increase in the money supply by the Bank of Canada? Do interest rates actually increase at the margin as a reaction to higher deficits? Is consumer spending or investment spending actually deterred or crowded out? While the answers depend upon the exact situation at the time, some generalizations can be made:

- In a fully employed economy, extra federal deficit financing will crowd out some private borrowing and ultimately some private spending.
- In an underemployed economy, the degree of crowding out depends upon the amount of financial and real slack in the economic system.
- It is difficult to evaluate the extent of crowding out in an economy when both high unemployment and high inflation occur simultaneously, since high rates of inflation tend to be associated with high interest rates, which themselves are often used as a measure of the crowding out effect.
- The needs of the federal government, which is Canada's prime borrower, will be met by the financial community at a better price than for, and usually with priority over, other borrowers. The reality is that there is a queuing process for loanable funds, and private sector borrowing will tend to be met after public needs are satisfied because of the insensitivity of public borrowing to higher interest rates.
- If crowding out is defined as the unavailability of loanable funds at any price, the crowding out syndrome has no meaning as long as a central bank keeps the money supply growing at a sufficiently high rate in relation to inflation so that real borrowing demands can be met. Alternatively, if crowding out is defined as the availability of funds but at an unacceptably high price, then crowding out could occur even in a seriously underemployed economy when it is simultaneously suffering from high inflation and high unemployment.
- The method for evaluating the crowding out effect depends very

much on the state of the economy at the moment in terms of both real variables—such as unemployment, capacity utilization, and investment intentions—and financial variables; that is, the supply and availability of credit at a particular price, and the rate of inflation.

With the available data, it is difficult to argue that the growing size of government deficits in post-1975 environment was the reason for weak private spending and borrowing.

Crowding Out and the Special Financing Privileges of the Federal Government

The federal government is the prime borrower in Canada; the Bank of Canada, which has the sole right of note issue, operates as the government's fiscal agent. In addition to its premier position in the financial community, the federal government has access to a number of other special privileges that aid it in its financing, including the issuance of Canada Savings Bonds, made possible because only a national government could accept such a liquidity risk, and treasury bills, which are required to fill the mandatory secondary reserves of the chartered banks. It is an important question whether these special privileges make substantially more difficult the financing of provincial governments and their agencies as well as the financing of the private sector. In this sense, the crowding out argument implies substantial increases in the price of funds available to these other sectors.

Canada Savings Bonds were a combined outgrowth of the savings certificates issued largely to school children during the second world war and the victory loan issues of that same period. They were introduced immediately after the war as a vehicle for individual savings that could be redeemed at any time at face value plus interest. Since that time, however, they have become the principal financing instrument of the federal government and by the mid-1970s they comprised 74 per cent of the outstanding national debt held by the general public. The bonds, which were formerly mainly for small savers, now attract investments of up to $25,000 per person per issue and can be included in trusts and estates. Canada Savings Bond issues continue, however, to be payable on demand, and thus the federal government is in a very difficult position in a period of rapidly rising interest rates. This happened particularly with the 1971 issue, when a major proportion of outstanding bonds were redeemed and new ones were issued at higher interest rates. The result was a vast increase in the interest cost to the

20

federal government that would have been delayed had the debt not been subject to demand repayment.

The existence of such personal investment opportunities in Canada Savings Bonds has resulted in some drying up of individual investments in corporate, provincial, and municipal securities. The individual investor of moderate means prefers the credit standing of the federal government plus the liquidity features of instant cash on demand. Other borrowers issuing medium-term (say, ten-year) debt could not compete in terms of either liquidity or financial standing. As a consequence, the Canada Saving Bond is the riskless *numéraire* in the Canadian capital market.

Another special privilege of the federal government lies in its ability, through the Bank of Canada, to increase the secondary reserve requirements of the chartered banks when additional funds are needed. According to the Bank Act, chartered bank secondary reserves must be invested in federal government treasury bills or day-to-day loans, which are short-term loans to investment dealers usually backed by treasury bills or short-term government of Canada securities. This means that every Canadian dollar deposited with the chartered banks is partially diverted to government financing through the secondary reserve requirement, a form of selective credit control. This is, indeed, a valuable privilege and one that has on occasion proved extremely worth while. But it does have the additional effect of making it more difficult and more expensive for the provincial governments to issue short-term bills similar to federal treasury bills, for such issues are not acceptable as chartered bank secondary reserves. In effect, every increment in the secondary reserve requirement crowds out private and other public financing from the banks.

In summary, the secondary reserve requirements imposed on the chartered banks are a valuable credit-rationing tool that the Bank of Canada alters from time to time to achieve selective credit objectives. Increases or decreases in required secondary reserves have no impact on the money supply unless they are accompanied by measures that also affect primary reserves. We would argue, however, that the definition of secondary reserves could be broadened to include short-term provincial securities. Even with this broadening of short-term assets, this selective credit control device would work precisely as before.

Conclusion

This chapter has stressed the relationship between monetarism as a theoretical doctrine and monetarism as a series of economic policies. The two concepts cannot easily be divided from one another, nor can the implications of monetarism for the economy easily be distinguished from the effects of macroeconomic policy measures. But the substantial changes that have occurred in monetary policy since 1975 seem to extend beyond the obvious insertion of a new monetary aggregate target system.

As this chapter emphasized, one big difference between monetarism and the more interventionist neo-Keynesian approach relates to the issue of stabilization policy and the inherent stability, or lack of stability, in an economy. Our assessment is that behind the shift to the monetarist policy stance is the motivating political reality that the Bank could, if it chose to do so, almost completely shun adverse public reaction as long as it fostered stability through the desired growth of the money stock. For example, while in the following chapters we take exception to the Bank's style of foreign exchange rate intervention, the Bank could have chosen to ignore completely the foreign exchange market effects on the Canadian economy. Such a lack of interest would have been completely consistent with both monetarist theory and the Bank's early pronouncements in 1975 and 1976 not to become preoccupied with a defence of the Canadian dollar.

The following chapter shifts the focus from monetarist theory to monetarist practice in Canada since 1975. As the chapter indicates, the monetary policies pursued in the second half of the decade could not completely satisfy a "pure monetarist," since the Bank did practice deliberate foreign exchange intervention.

22

Canada's Monetarist Counter-Revolution

3

In September 1975 the Governor of the Bank of Canada, Gerald Bouey, announced to the Canadian public in a speech in Saskatoon that a significant alteration had taken place in monetary strategy.

> On previous occasions we have generally ended up, for all sorts of plausible short-term reasons, by turning economic recovery into an inflationary boom. This time around, it seems to me, we would be well advised to take a long look backwards at where we have been making our mistakes. . . . You can be confident that the Bank of Canada will permit a rate of monetary expansion that by any reasonable standard is sufficient to meet the needs of a good economic recovery with some moderation in the pace of inflation."[1]

No longer would the Bank become so overcommitted to short-term economic problems that it lost sight of important long-term objectives. High inflation was the obvious number one problem in 1975 as the rate of increase in consumer prices accelerated to just under 11 per cent in both 1974 and 1975. To help moderate inflation Mr. Bouey stated that the Bank would attempt to lower progressively the rate of increase in the money supply. From then on money supply growth rates were officially adopted as the instruments for achieving lower inflation.

In addition to specific money supply targets, the Bank informed the public that it should be prepared to expect the possibility of wider swings in interest rates and the value of the Canadian dollar, since the Bank was no longer committed in the same way to evening out interest rate and exchange rate variations. The Bank candidly admitted that the attempts to contain the external value of the Canadian dollar in the early 1970s by keeping Canada's interest rate structure relatively low resulted in too-rapid growth in the money supply and set the stage for the higher inflation rates of the mid-1970s.[2]

The strategy of deliberately setting targets for money supply growth rates, rather than interest rates and credit conditions, is often labelled "monetarist." But, in fact, the meaning of monetarism is much more encompassing. The new strategy, as discussed in this study, has theoretical and practical implications for the proper role of economic stabilization policies, the inherent stability of the economy, and the inflation process.

The new monetary strategy was accompanied by important changes in fiscal policy as well as the imposition of a mandatory wage, price, and profit control programme. The stated fiscal policy goals were to restrain federal government spending with the objective of reducing its share of GNP. While this was to be a longer-term objective, in fact it immediately affected the budgets of government departments, and other levels of government also embraced this doctrine of fiscal restraint. The controls programme was set up and monitored by the new Anti-Inflation Board, which had a three-year mandate. During that time, the inflation rate and wage increases were to decline progressively to below annual increases of 6 per cent and 4 per cent respectively. The inflation objectives were not, of course, attained, though money wage settlements did de-escalate in fairly close conformity with the guidelines.

The immediate Bank of Canada policy was to reduce gradually the growth rate in the money supply. It was thought that in time this strategy would result in a lower inflation rate in Canada. For this purpose the Bank defined the money supply as demand deposits in the chartered banks and currency in the hands of the public, the definition of the money supply commonly referred to as M1. Other definitions of the money supply include a broader spectrum of bank and non-bank deposits, but the Bank concluded on the basis of its own empirical studies that the narrow M1 version was the appropriate target variable. The various money supply definitions and their values and growth rates since 1967 are shown in Table 3-1. A discussion of the technical problems of setting money supply targets is set out in Appendix A.

Ironically, the instrument chosen to achieve the money supply targets was short-term interest rates, which were previously an intermediate objective. That is, in the post-1975 environment, short-term interest rates have been altered through open market operations to achieve stated money supply targets. In contrast, the money supply in the past was varied to achieve interest rate objectives—or the credit conditions goal. In the final analysis, in both pre- and post-1975, these monetary measures were directed towards general economic goals such as em-

TABLE 3-1
MONETARY AGGREGATES AND THEIR GROWTH RATES, 1967-78

	M1 — Currency and demand deposits		M1B — Currency and all chequable deposits		M2 — Currency and all chequable notice and term deposits		M3 — Currency plus total privately held chartered bank deposits		Currency and privately held Canadian dollar deposits	
	Amount	Growth	Amount	Growth	Amount	Growth	Amount	Growth	Amount	Growth
	($ Millions)	(%)	($ Millions)	(%)	($ Millions)	(%)	($ Millions)	(%)	($ Millions)	(%)
1967	7,975	9.7	16,635	—	—	—	—	—	22,240	12.2
1968	8,323	4.4	15,797	− 5.0	21,778	—	—	—	25,192	13.3
1969	8,919	7.2	15,447	− 2.2	24,044	10.4	—	—	27,615	9.6
1970	9,117	2.2	14,810	− 4.1	25,680	6.8	32,275	—	29,122	5.5
1971	10,275	12.7	16,170	9.2	28,854	12.4	35,593	10.3	33,315	14.4
1972	11,744	14.3	18,216	12.7	31,899	10.6	40,577	14.0	39,203	17.7
1973	13,444	14.5	20,378	11.9	36,416	14.2	46,637	14.9	44,462	13.4
1974	14,729	9.6	21,571	5.9	43,726	20.1	58,187	24.8	53,263	19.8
1975	16,728	13.6	23,649	9.6	50,291	15.0	66,785	14.8	62,635	17.6
1976	18,082	8.1	25,114	6.2	56,597	12.5	79,034	18.3	73,273	17.0
1977	19,590	8.3	26,907	7.1	64,538	14.0	91,529	15.8	84,452	15.3
1978	21,569	10.1	29,295	8.9	71,436	10.7	104,060	13.7	94,515	11.9

Source: Department of Finance, *Economic Review* (April 1979), p. 224.

TABLE 3-2
MONEY SUPPLY GROWTH RATES AND TARGETS, 1975-79

	Actual Money Supply (M1-S/A)[a]	Annualized Growth Rates From			Targets		POLICY TARGET STATEMENT
		Base Quarter	Previous Quarter	Year Earlier	High	Low	
	($ Millions)	(Per cent)			($ Millions)		
1975 1Q	15,685		24.3	9.7			
2Q	16,312	17.1	17.0	8.9			
3Q	16,937	21.9	16.2	14.8	16,861	16,676	November, 1976—10 to 15 per cent growth over 3 months-centred average May 1975 base.[b]
4Q	17,978	12.3	27.0	21.0	17,462	17,078	
1976 1Q	17,761	10.0	−4.8	13.2	18,082	17,490	
2Q	17,905	9.5	3.3	9.8	18,725	17,911	
3Q	18,238		7.6	7.7	19,390	18,343	
4Q	18,427	6.4	4.2	2.5	19,116	18,662	August 24/76—8 to 12 per cent growth over 3 months centred average March 1976 base.[c]
1977 1Q	18,817	7.0	8.7	5.9	19,666	19,024	
2Q	19,356	8.0	12.0	8.1	20,231	19,394	
3Q	19,825	8.3	10.0	8.7	20,812	19,771	
4Q	20,360	9.6	11.3	10.5	20,462	20,152	October 7/77—7 to 11 per cent growth over June 1977 base and 2 per cent tolerance band.[c]
1978 1Q	20,651	8.3	5.8	9.7	21,003	20,496	
2Q	21,137	8.7	9.8	9.2	21,558	20,846	
3Q	21,862	9.8	4.4	10.3	22,128	21,201	
4Q	22,625	13.5	14.7	11.1	22,236	21,897	September 11/78—6 to 10 per cent growth over June 1978 base and 2 per cent tolerance band.[c]
1979 1Q	22,259	6.5	−1.6	7.8	22,772	22,218	

[a] M1 includes demand deposits at banks plus publicly held currency. [b] *Bank of Canada Review*, November 1976.
[c] Bank of Canada press release; August 24, 1976; October 7; 1977; and September 11, 1978.

ployment creation, price stability, economic growth, and a viable balance of payments.

For example, in the pre-1975 period, when it was thought that higher interest rates were required to reduce the growth in investment, inventory accumulation, or consumer spending, the money supply variable was acted upon directly either through a slowing of its growth rate or an actual contraction of the money supply. In the post-1975 period, when a lower money supply growth rate was required to lower nominal GNP growth and presumably lower inflation, then the Bank raised short-term interest rates to achieve its goal of economizing on demand deposits and currency in circulation to moderate the growth of the M1 money supply.

As Table 3-1 indicates, the Bank was rather successful in achieving its goal. Whereas M1 advanced very rapidly in four out of the five years between 1971 and 1975, considerable deceleration towards the target rate of money supply growth occurred in 1976 and 1977, and during 1978 the pace of growth of the money supply increased only moderately (Table 3-2). Other official definitions of the money supply showed a variety of growth rates since 1975, though targets for them were not formally set by the Bank of Canada. The figures for 1978 indicate a trend towards deceleration, particularly with the broader M2 and M3 measures of the money supply. Thus on the basis of the monetary targets and the actual money supply growth rates since 1975, the Bank had achieved its stated objectives. But the real effects on the economy cannot be regarded as successful.

The Economic Effects of Monetarism in Canada, 1975–79

The economic performance of the Canadian economy was profoundly affected by the Bank's adoption of monetarism. The effects were felt in both the international and the domestic areas. In the international arena, the adoption of monetarism initially allowed the Bank to ignore the effects of the exchange rate on output and inflation. But by 1978 major support actions in foreign exchange markets were undertaken, violating monetarist principles. In the domestic arena, there were major negative effects on the rate of unemployment, on the ability of the economy to grow, and on the rate of inflation.

The Effects of Ignoring the Exchange Rate

The deterioration in Canada's international payments situation is evident in Table 3-3. In the early 1970s Canada had achieved a rough balance in its current account on international transactions. In 1974,

TABLE 3-3
CANADA'S BALANCE OF PAYMENTS, 1970-79

	1970	1973	1974	1975	1976	1977	1978	1979[a]
				($ Billions)				
Current transactions								
Merchandise exports	16.9	25.5	32.6	33.5	38.1	44.6	52.4	63.4
Merchandise imports	13.9	22.7	30.9	34.0	36.8	41.7	48.9	61.2
BALANCE ON TRADE IN GOODS	3.1	2.8	1.7	−0.5	1.3	2.9	3.5	2.2
Services exports	4.2	5.2	6.4	6.9	7.6	8.1	9.5	11.4
Services imports	6.3	8.2	10.1	11.6	13.2	15.5	18.3	20.8
(of which interest and dividend abroad were)	(1.5)	(2.0)	(2.4)	(2.9)	(3.3)	(4.3)	(5.4)	
BALANCE ON TRADE IN SERVICES	−2.1	−3.0	−3.7	−4.7	−5.6	−7.4	−8.8	−9.4
Net transfers	0.1	0.3	0.6	0.4	0.5	0.4	—	0.4
CURRENT ACCOUNT BALANCE	1.1	0.1	−1.4	−4.8	−3.8	−4.1	−5.3	−6.8
Capital transactions								
Net long-term capital	1.0	0.6	1.0	3.9	7.9	4.6	3.5	
Net short-term capital	−0.2	−0.5	1.3	1.6	0.1	0.9	0.3	
TOTAL NET CAPITAL	0.8	0.1	2.3	5.5	8.0	5.5	3.8	
Errors and ommissions	−0.4	−0.6	−0.8	−1.2	−3.7	−2.7	−1.8	

[a] Forecast figures.

Source: Actual data from *Bank of Canada Review* (May 1979), Tables 68 and 70. Forecast data from Toronto-Dominion Bank, *Canada's Business Climate* (Winter 1979), and subsequent revisions.

however, the Canadian dollar proceeded to rise sharply in the first few months of the year to just below U.S. $1.05. The result was that for the remainder of that year the current account deficit continued to increase so that by the first quarter of 1975 it had reached an annual rate of $5 billion. The deficit hovered around $4 billion in 1976 and 1977 and then rose dramatically to a predicted $7 billion in 1979.

For most of the time from 1974 through 1976 the Canadian dollar traded above par with the U.S. dollar and Canada's inflation and wage cost performance deteriorated sharply compared with that in the United States. It was not until late 1978 that Canada's inflation and wage cost increases fell marginally below those in the United States. In absolute terms, the 20 per cent depreciation of the Canadian relative to the U.S. dollar brought costs of production back to a competitive level with those in the United States (Table 3-4).

After interest rates peaked in both Canada and the United States in

TABLE 3-4
ESTIMATED HOURLY COMPENSATION OF PRODUCTION
WORKERS IN MANUFACTURING[a], TEN COUNTRIES,
SELECTED YEARS, 1960-78

	1960	1965	1970	1977	June 1978
	($ U.S.)				
United States	2.67(1)[b]	3.14	4.19	7.60	8.26(5)
Canada[c]	2.13(2)	2.28	3.46	7.40	7.54(6)
Japan	.26(10)	.48	.99	3.97	5.65(9)
Belgium	.83(4)	1.32	2.08	8.40	9.88(2)
France	.83(5)	1.24	1.74	5.40	6.90(7)
Germany	.83(6)	1.41	2.33	7.73	9.18(4)
Italy	.63(9)	1.13	1.77	5.17	6.18(8)
Netherlands	.68(8)	1.24	2.14	8.21	9.62(3)
Sweden	1.20(3)	1.86	2.95	8.22	9.88(1)
United Kingdom	.83(7)	1.15	1.48	3.34	4.24(10)

[a] Total compensation per hour worked is estimated by adjusting average hourly earnings for items of direct pay not included in earnings and for employer expenditures for social security and contractual and private insurance programs and for other labour taxes.

[b] The figures in parenthesis indicate rank from high to low.

[c] The exchange value of the Canadian dollar in June of 1978 was U.S. $0.89.

Source: U.S. Department of Labor, Bureau of Labor Statistics, Office of Productivity and Technology, Division of Foreign Labor Statistics and Trade.

late 1974, they declined rapidly in the United States. In Canada they fell much more slowly, and in mid-1975 the Bank again moved to raise interest rates. U.S. rates remained at relatively low levels. The result was that in 1976 interest rates in Canada were 4 percentage points higher than those in the United States on short-term money market paper and securities. In addition, a large differential between Canadian and U.S. yields on longer-term bonds opened up. The high Canadian interest rates on the longer-term securities were one of the main causes of the sharp inflow of long-term capital in the form of borrowed funds during 1976. That borrowing abroad was principally regarded as the cause of the very strong Canadian dollar in the face of a sharply deteriorating current account in Canada's international payments situation. Thus monetary policy was the key cause of excessive borrowing abroad; government authorities also encouraged such an inflow through other actions.

As a result of such capital inflows the Canadian economy developed a continuing large current account deficit. The unnecessarily high exchange rate between 1974 and 1976 plus some further deterioration in wage competitiveness meant that Canada's manufacturing and some other industries became less competitive not only in international markets, but also in the domestic market. The current account deficit was exacerbated by the large and growing interest payments that were required each year to service the funds borrowed abroad. Further borrowing abroad in 1976 to finance the current account deficit led to interest payments that were about $0.5 billion higher in 1977 and subsequent years. In addition, in 1977 and 1978 the depreciation of the Canadian dollar added to the cost of interest payments abroad, which were largely denominated in U.S. dollars. This is strikingly apparent in the services transactions deficit of the current account, which stood at less than $3 billion in 1973 and rose to about $8.8 billion in 1978 (Table 3-3).

With each succeeding yearly current account deficit, Canada fell more into debt internationally. In turn, this increased debt required higher interest payments abroad in following years, contributing to even larger current account deficits. What happened in the post-1975 era in Canada is a clear example of the interaction of international borrowing and the deepening of current account deficits. This vicious circle seemed to be ignored by the Bank of Canada and government policymakers in general until 1978 when financing concerns became prominent. Even then Ottawa seemed to be more concerned about financing the existing current account deficit than about either the size

30

of the deficit or developing policies to reduce it. Both the government and the Bank have continued to be remarkably silent over the problems of future debt servicing, the size of the current account deficit that was likely to result, and their interaction.[3]

The Canadian government refused, particularly in 1976, to offset the massive international borrowings through accumulations of exchange reserves. As a result these capital inflows effectively set an inappropriately high level for the Canadian dollar that forced Canada into a compensating current account deficit. If the high level of foreign borrowings can be attributed to monetary policy since 1975 then it is clear that that policy was inappropriate in terms of Canada's balance of payments goals. The Bank's policies of first raising Canadian interest rates above U.S. rates to fight inflation in 1976, then in 1978 and 1979 raising domestic interest rates in order to finance the current account deficit only ensured that the current account deficit would persist. That is, the Bank's preoccupation with the need to finance the deficit, not to cure it, resulted in even greater deficits because the exchange rate was first kept at too high a level and second because interest payments abroad became onerous when the dollar finally declined to a realistic level.

The Effects on the Domestic Economy of Monetarist Economic Policies

In a world in which high unemployment and high inflation coincide rather than appear sequentially, it is difficult to link particular economic policies with their impact on the economy and to label those policies accurately. Further distinctions between the effects of monetary and fiscal policies are difficult to make as both are used in the management of Canada's economy. Moreover, economic measures are supposedly co-ordinated and, in addition, the Minister of Finance has an ultimate veto on Bank actions that are inconsistent with government objectives.

Canada's post-1975 monetary policy became known as one of "gradualism." But while it is somewhat dangerous to select one element in a mix of stabilization policies to consider whether or not that part of the total package of policies is gradualistic, stimulative, or something else, monetary policy was apparently more heavy handed than gradualistic. The label also refers to the manner in which the policies were applied rather than to the effects of the policies, which were hardly gradual and led to a post-depression high unemployment rate and a generally stagnating economy performing well below its

31

potential. As a comparison, over the ten-year interval from 1963 to 1973, the average annual real growth rate of the economy was 5.7 per cent. The rate then fell drastically to 1.3 per cent in 1975, 5.5 per cent in 1976, 2.7 per cent in 1977, and 3.4 per cent in 1978. Most private economic forecasters suggested in early 1979 that the Canadian economy would grow by about 3 per cent in 1979.

When the government and the Bank ushered in the new policy framework, at worst a falling off of economic growth and higher unemployment might have been expected as inflation moderated. But despite the help of the Anti-Inflation Board and the de-escalation of money wage settlements, the consumer price picture never truly improved. If the sum of the unemployment and inflation rates were used as a crude index of national economic discomfort, total discomfort would be seen to have remained relatively unchanged between 1975 and 1978. In 1975 the consumer price index rose 10.8 per cent and the unemployment rate averaged 6.9 per cent. In 1978 consumer prices rose 9 per cent, while the unemployment rate averaged 8.2 per cent. There was, therefore, a trade-off: the inflation rate declined slightly, but unemployment increased substantially.[4]

Another related problem that developed in this period was the rising federal government deficit, which soared to about $12 billion in fiscal 1978/79. This was the result of both the lagging domestic economy with its rising unemployment and persistent inflation and fiscal measures such as the introduction of indexed tax brackets and personal income tax exemptions and the inflation indexing of social assistance payments.

Despite the huge increase in government deficits since 1974, there was some debate about whether fiscal policy was too expansive or not expansive enough. Some claimed that fiscal expansion from Ottawa was crowding out private demand because it was contributing to higher interest rates. Others argued that, on the contrary, the expansive fiscal measures introduced after 1975 were much too meagre to reduce the high unemployment levels. The government of Ontario entered the debate in a combative manner. Their position was that fiscal policy was indeed very stimulative but the self-correcting mechanism expected to promote stronger economic activity and reduce the budget deficit over time was inadequate. They backed up their argument with their own estimates of a full-employment position for the budget of Canada (Table 3-5). In restrospect it now appears that stronger economic growth did not yield sufficiently increased revenues and reduced expenditures to markedly reduce government deficits.

32

TABLE 3-5

ONTARIO ESTIMATES OF CANADA'S FULL-EMPLOYMENT BUDGET POSITION, 1971-77

	1971	1972	1973	1974	1975	1976	1977
				($ Millions)			
National Accounts surplus or (deficit)	(145)	(566)	387	1083	(3551)	(2879)	(6944)
Full employment surplus or (deficit)	290	(188)	(205)	(527)	(1852)	(1029)	(3564)[a]
							(5344)

[a] The differences between these two figures for 1977 are related to methodology and assumptions. The lower figure derives from the traditional method of calculation; the higher figure, from the alternative method, which assumes a higher full-employment unemployment rate than in the former case.

Source: Ministry of Treasury, Economics and Intergovernmental Affairs, *Reassessing the Scope for Fiscal Policy in Canada*, Staff Paper 15 (Toronto, n.d.).

The full-employment measure of a budget differs from the actual recorded deficit or surplus through calculation of the hypothetical position of where the budget would be if the economy were fully employed. A fully employed economy would require fewer federal government transfers to support the poor and unemployed, and federal revenues would in principle be higher as a result of a stronger economy. Fiscal policy then could be judged by changes in the full-employment budget position over various periods. If in 1979, for example, Canada's estimated full-employment budget were in surplus, while in 1978 it had been in deficit, the 1979 budget would be regarded as more restrictive for the economy than the 1978 budget. This measure allows for the automatic feedback effect on the economy of federal revenues and expenditures, and thus the fiscal impact of a budget can be evaluted in terms of discretionary changes alone rather than in terms of the automatic effects on the economy as the degree of economic slack predictably alters revenues and expenditures.

What surprised many observers about the Ontario estimates was that, even utilizing a full-employment assumption, the federal budget would have recorded a substantial deficit in 1977, ranging between $3.6 billion and $5.3 billion. Thus a stronger economy would not in itself have eliminated the 1977 budget deficit. Clearly federal revenues no longer expand more rapidly than the growth of the economy; that is, the elasticity of Ottawa's revenue system was reduced sharply after the 1974-75 fiscal year. As well, there is the additional reality that high unemployment and the indexed compensation and social assistance payments make it difficult for federal expenditures to grow much below the nominal GNP growth rate.

Canada was not alone in experiencing economic difficulties after 1975, but there were some differences. In 1978 the inflation rate, though similar to that in the United States, tended to be nearly double the rate in Germany and Japan. But in terms of growth rates and employment generation, comparisons with other industrial nations have little meaning, since Canada's full-capacity growth rate was relatively high. Still, by the end of 1978 Canada recorded the highest unemployment rate among the major trading nations, though it must be remembered that, unlike certain European countries, Canada did not have a safety valve of foreign labour that could be repatriated when economic conditions worsened. Canada's record of job expansion over this period was much better than that in other industrial nations, but nevertheless it fell to an average annual rate of 2.6 per cent between 1975 and 1978 compared with 3.7 per cent in the previous four years.

34

The poor performance of the economy over the four years ending in 1978 stands in contrast to the American experience. Whereas the United States averaged a 4.8 per cent real growth rate in the 1975-78 period, Canada achieved less than a 3 per cent average growth rate, even though Canada's economic potential was rising at a faster pace than that in the United States. United States unemployment declined from a 9 per cent peak in 1975 to average about 6 per cent by 1978. In Canada the direction was the reverse, with the unemployment rate moving up from 5.5 per cent in 1974 to a high of 8.6 per cent in 1978. These divergent trends were partly a reflection of underlying demand conditions in the two economies. Aggregate demand was weak in Canada, but strong in the United States.

Criticisms of Monetarism

By 1979 Canadian policymakers were entrapped by a series of difficulties inherited from 1978 and the three preceding years. The federal government's deficit was growing despite spending restraint and political pressure to reduce it, and any further increase would have been perceived to have added to inflation and further weaken the dollar. The dollar traded in 1978 at about U.S. $.85 and fell to a low of U.S. $.83 early in 1979 despite massive intervention. Interest rates could not be kept low to encourage the expansion of real investment as this too would have weakened the dollar and added to inflation; indeed, the Bank had increased rates in step with rises in U.S. rates. At this point the Bank of Canada was criticized by both its monetarist supporters and its non-monetarist critics.

Monetarists tended to be critical of the direct foreign exchange intervention. Some argued that the government was financing an unwarranted large deficit in international markets. Others noted that, while the Bank had rejected fixed exchange rates and exchange rate intervention, in the crunch that institution had intervened, abandoning an important tenet of monetarist ideology.[5]

Non-monetarists tended to be critical on two grounds. The acceptance of higher interest rates in 1978 was deemed to be unnecessary in view of the poor economic prospects facing the economy in 1978 and 1979. As well, they argued that once the dollar stabilized at a lower level of about U.S. $.85, moderate domestic labour cost increases would play a more dominant role in containing Canada's inflation rate below that of the United States. Some also argued that the risk of further depreciation of the Canadian dollar from the U.S. $.85 level was limited, and that it was more a question of politics than economics that prompted the exchange rate intervention. Observers were also critical of the government's and the Bank's support actions in two other ways. First, it was thought that the Minister of Finance was stretching the truth when he repeatedly stated that direct support for the dollar represented nothing more than normal "smoothing operations" by the Exchange Fund when indeed in late 1978 and early 1979 an "exchange crisis" existed. Second, critics also claimed that the Bank and the government managed the support action ineptly in 1978—that their borrowings were clearly defensive reactions rather than the needed aggressive actions.

Early in the exchange crisis of 1978-79, the federal government's borrowings in New York were relatively small compared with the amounts required to be effective. By early 1979, however, the incremental borrowings amounted to over $5 billion; in addition, lines of credit amounting to another U.S. $5.5 billion were established with Canadian and foreign banks. Such large amounts, together with the 1979 Iranian oil crisis and the strengthening of the U.S. dollar, appeared to have ended the exchange crisis, as the Canadian dollar increased in value to about U.S. $0.87 by April. But later adverse trade statistics and the release of exchange reserve statistics indicating large foreign exchange intervention in May again weakened the value of the dollar to about U.S. $0.85 in June 1979.

In reality it must be recognized that there is no such thing as a freely floating exchange rate as long as the Bank sets short-term interest rates with a view to maintaining a particular external value of the currency. Our criticism of the Bank in this regard is not related to exchange rate intervention per se. Instead, our concern is with the style of exchange rate management between 1975 and 1978. By deliberately forcing up Canada's exchange rate in 1976 through high interest rates, the Bank set in motion a series of events that locked Canada into long-term permanently high current account deficits and slow real economic growth. The 1976 policies forestalled the inevitable adjustment of the dollar to a more realistic level. After the initial policy error the Bank should have expected a sharp decline in the value of the dollar and have been prepared to move more forcefully when it began to fall. If one accepts that direct intervention was required, then the actual strategy of piecemeal foreign exchange intervention must be viewed as a failure.

Whether direct intervention was desirable or not, the authorities should have expected substantial currency runs on the dollar in response to its overvaluation in 1976 and subsequent high inflation. They

36

should have made preparations in 1976 that included the stocking up of exchange reserves in advance. This policy direction would have reduced the rise of the dollar in 1976 and prevented some of the subsequent speculation and the trail of inadequate support actions in 1978.

Conclusion

In early 1979 the Bank of Canada was still firmly committed to the money supply growth rate targets and parallel if not higher interest rates than in the United States to support the external value of the Canadian dollar. While a case can be made that Canada should maintain money supply targets, our assessment of monetary policy during the latter half of the 1970s indicates that the targets should not have been pursued dogmatically. These targets were upheld during the 1978-79 exchange crisis, though the principle of a freely fluctuating Canadian exchange rate was abandoned. But had it been necessary to support the exchange rate even further, money supply growth rates below the lower target limit would likely have been tolerated by the Bank. The Bank would probably not, however, have been as willing to forgo the targets on the upper limit to encourage the growth of the domestic economy, for it feared further inflation.

Although the Bank was preoccupied with reducing the rate of inflation, nevertheless inflation was of such a nature that it was unlikely to be affected by monetary policy. Our analysis indicates that monetary policy objectives must be reformulated in light of the structural aspects of inflation. That is, it makes little sense to restrict economic growth in Canada when tight money is having only a minimal impact on the underlying rate of inflation because of the stubborn insensitivity of money wages and energy and food prices to monetary conditions. Although the money supply targets are consistent with the long-run view that inflation is a monetary phenomenon, the inflation Canada has experienced since 1973, and which appears likely to continue into the 1980s, cannot be described as a monetary inflation. Other policies should be pursued to reduce the effects of structural inflation. In the following chapters, several other policy options are considered. While this study in itself does not point to the definitive policy mix, it is clear that, without other anti-inflationary measures, the present monetary targets will restrict real economic growth significantly below potential rates. Additional policy options are considered in the context of structural inflation in the following chapter.

Structural Inflation

4

Why did Canada's inflation in the 1970s fail to moderate in response to the high level of unemployment? In the past, the trade-off between inflation and unemployment, as predicted by the Phillips curve, would have returned the rate of inflation back to the 3 per cent to 4 per cent range when unemployment exceeded 6 per cent.[1] Yet in 1978, when the unemployment rate averaged 8.4 per cent, the rate of increase in the consumer price index in Canada was 9 per cent (see Table A-1).

A number of explanations were advanced for the worsening response of domestic inflation to the recorded unemployment rate.

- The "structural unemployment" explanation states that the rate of unemployment that could be regarded as "full employment" for the Canadian economy increased markedly in the 1970s because of a rapidly growing "young" labour force and because of the significant improvements in the benefits paid under the unemployment insurance compensation scheme.

- The "inflationary expectations" explanation contends that because of years of high inflation, inflationary expectations, which affect the wage-setting process directly and the price-setting mechanism indirectly, rose progressively and remained at a high level.

- The "special factors" explanation argues that a series of special factors occurred that were external to the Canadian economy and could not be overcome domestically: high food price increases from 1977 to 1979, the continuing pressure on energy prices from 1973 onward, and the effects of the substantial depreciation of the Canadian dollar after 1976.

- The "broad monetarist" position is that the rapid increases that occurred in the broadly defined money supply were inflationary compared with the slower recorded growth rate in the narrowly defined money supply, M1 (see Tables A-1 and A-2).

None of these explanations individually provides a complete or adequate explanation of Canada's continuing inflation and the limited public policy options as both inflation and unemployment worsened; that is, as the Phillips curve shifted outward. Each of the four explanations seems only a partial explanation. Though demographic changes shifted the full-employment zone to a higher recorded unemployment rate in the late 1970s, there was a substantial excess supply of labour even when the rate was adjusted for the rapid increase in new entrants. And, while we would not disagree that inflationary expectations rose in Canada in the 1970s, the acceptance of that position does not go far enough to explain the worsening inflation picture. How are such expectations formed? How can they be altered? As well, there were special factors that shocked Canada's price structure at various times during the period, but two of the special factors—food inflation and currency depreciation related inflation—were relatively short term, while the effect of energy price increases have been wrongly dismissed by many economists as nothing more than a substantial shift in relative prices. Conventional economic principles would link rising inflationary expectations to these special factors, though the linkage mechanism is somewhat obscure. Equally untenable in our view is the "broad" monetarist position, because of its inability to account for the high inflation of the late 1970s despite a moderation in the growth of the broad money supply. Thus we are still without a comprehensive explanation of inflation. In the next section, we examine the issue in detail in an attempt to provide a convincing reason why inflation did not moderate as unemployment rose and why monetary policy failed to alleviate the persistent difficulties.

Explaining Inflation

An eclectic short-run view of the inflation mechanism must begin with the acknowledgement that the recorded rate of Canadian inflation has a foreign and domestic component. The external component is, of course, related to the international prices that affect Canada's terms of trade and movements in the exchange rate at least in the short run. The domestic inflation component depends upon the cyclical movement in money wages, price markups, and labour productivity in the private sector and money wage and salary increases in the public sector. Domestic inflationary expectations enter the picture through their impact on money wage increases. Thus a complete and short-run model of wage-price dynamics in Canada must take into account the tightness of the labour market and inflationary expectations as well as the cyclical position of the Canadian economy. Since the unemployment rate is regarded as a reasonable business cycle indicator, the entire inflation determination model can collapse into an explanation dependent upon three items: the unemployment rate, inflationary expectations, and foreign inflation.[2]

Ignoring the effects of foreign inflation, the inflation theory we have just sketched is compatible with a modified Phillips curve explanation; that is, there exists a hypothetical inverse relationship between unemployment and inflation.[3] In fact, the two dimensional inflation-unemployment trade-off (the Phillips curve) is three dimensional in that shifts in inflationary expectations will in themselves alter the position of the Phillips curve. This is why economists refer to a family of Phillips curves rather than to a single schedule representing only one series of inflation-unemployment options. But while this model appears plausible, it still fails to explain adequately the current inflation-unemployment dilemma.

Our explanation is more comprehensive. We maintain that the 1970s inflation had an additional structural element that worsened the trade-offs in a manner somewhat similar to rising inflationary expectations, though as the 1970s progressed the worsening of the trade-off option may be as much the result of structural factors as of increased inflationary expectations. Indeed, for policy, the structural explanation must be treated separately from the inflationary expectations explanation, though they appear similar in many ways, because in the current circumstances a reduction in inflationary expectations might not return the Canadian economy to the lower rates of inflation experienced in the past when unemployment was as high.

Basically, the array of Phillips curves that theoretically provide for a range of interaction between unemployment, inflation, and inflationary expectations is missing a structural variable. The absence of that variable leaves the explanation of the relationship between current inflation and unemployment devoid of much the informed public regards as realistic. The inclusion of a structural variable in the 1970s would seemingly have shifted the range of inflation and unemployment trade-off curves outward, narrowing the policy options even further. For example, if an unemployment rate of 6 per cent and an inflation rate of 6 per cent combined with inflationary expectations of 5 per cent, rising structural inflation would lead to a worsening in the trade-off even if inflationary expectations remained constant at the 5 per cent level.

At this point it is necessary to define more precisely what is meant

40

by structural inflation, though it will become clear to the reader that it is almost easier to describe the concept in terms of what it is not rather than what it represents. The dominant feature of inflation that can be described as structural is that some part of the recorded rate of inflation is clearly independent of cyclical changes in the economy, even allowing for normal lags. Since economic stabilization measures are thought to operate primarily through their direct influence on the economy's short-term or cyclical performance—that is, aggregate demand—the smaller the impact demand-management policies have on inflation, the greater the degree to which such inflation may be described as structural. That is, structural inflation does not normally originate either in cyclical or monetary phenomena.[4]

The natural counterpart to structural inflation is the concept of structural unemployment. Structural unemployment represents long-run unemployment that cannot be reduced by short-term economic improvements, since it exists because of labour market bottlenecks, industrial, regional, or economic imbalances, or skilled labour shortages. Labour economists have long recognized that the policies appropriate for reducing cyclical unemployment are clearly different from policies needed to reduce long-term structural unemployment. In a similar manner, macroeconomic policies appropriate for containing cyclical inflation (aggregate demand policies) differ from the policies for containing inflation that appears insensitive to the cyclical position of the economy. And just as structural unemployment narrows policy options because it requires a higher unemployment rate to place downward pressures on inflation, an apparent rise in structural inflation limits policy options for the national authorities. That is, higher increases in unemployment may not dampen the inflation in the expected manner if the inflation has worsened for structural rather than cyclical reasons. This is an important aspect of our criticism of the demand-management policies of the late 1970s.

In the following discussion of policy, we distinguish between inflation associated with increasing inflationary expectations and that associated with worsening structural factors. For public policy purposes the inflationary pressures that are independent of the short-run movements of the economy should not be identified with inflationary expectations. Factors that have increased the amount of structural inflation in the 1970s are higher world energy prices, the gradualistic policy adopted by Canada to bring Canada's domestic energy prices up to world levels, and the policy of economic gradualism primarily associated with the monetarist counter-revolution.

41

Some economists would argue that what we identify as structural inflation would be more appropriately described as significant changes in relative prices. The problem with using that identification is that it is not helpful for policymakers. It is also the case that the economic literature stresses that relative price changes do not cause inflation. The usual diagnosis of the impact of significant relative price changes on the national inflation rate is that once the adjustment process has worked itself out, further inflation would be independent of those relative price movements that began the process. The argument is that the recorded increase in the rate of price hikes associated with a relative price change will be short-term or transitional. We argue that in the 1970s, the energy-related price effect cannot be regarded as "normally" transitional, and indeed rapid escalation of energy prices seems certain to continue in the 1980s.

In this regard, the Department of Finance identified important structural changes in the labour market in the 1970s that made it more difficult to bring down the rate of inflation: "The initial effect of the 1972-1974 price shocks was to directly raise the rate of inflation. This led to higher wage demands, partly because of attempts to maintain real wages and partly also because of expectations of future higher rates of inflation. The result was a secondary wage-price spiral."[5]

Of the four elements often cited as having played an external role in explaining the acceleration of inflation in the late 1970s, food prices and the depreciation of the Canadian dollar do not fall within our classification of structural factors, although both aggravated the inflation problem, since their effects must be regarded as relatively short term. Over the longer term, there is good reason to expect that food prices will rise at a rate that is relatively comparable with the general inflation rate and that the Canadian dollar will neither add to nor subtract from the general inflation picture. This, of course, was not the case over the shorter term.[6] But energy and wage inflation—the other two factors often cited—fall within our description of structural forces. While competitive forces play a role in both markets, the wage and energy effects on inflation in the 1970s operate in a structural way.

Since October 1973 when OPEC started raising their crude oil prices, prices for fuels in Canada have been rising with the intended goal of closing the gap between the Canadian and the world price. Ottawa felt that this strategy was necessary, since Canada is both an importer and an exporter of crude oil and petroleum products. Such a policy was also designed to foster energy conservation.

As a result of Canada's reaction to these largely external events, domestic crude oil prices have increased sharply. The federal government's strategy was to gradually increase oil prices to a comparable level with OPEC prices and at the same time to raise the price of Canadian-produced natural gas to that of its oil equivalent on a BTU basis. Thus the well-head price of domestic crude oil rose from $2.90 per barrel in 1972 to $13.75 per barrel on July 1, 1979. These price hikes have, of course, seriously affected the cost-of-living indexes in Canada not only directly through increases in the price of gasoline and heating oil but also indirectly through price increases for all industrial products that use significant amounts of energy.

Further price increases are imminent, though the oil-price gap will still not be closed. For example, in July of 1979 the delivered crude oil price into eastern Canada was about $14.70 per barrel. The average landed price of OPEC oil in eastern Canada was $24.80 per barrel in July, which left a federal subsidy or gap of about $10.10 per barrel. This contrasts with a subsidy or gap of $3 per barrel on July 1, 1978.

If it is assumed that domestic oil prices will increase annually by $4 per barrel between 1980 and 1985, then the average wellhead price ($16.25 per barrel in 1980) would rise to $36.25 per barrel by 1985. In a similar fashion, natural gas prices may be expected to rise sharply in order to maintain their oil equivalent price. If one assumes that every $1 per barrel increase translates into a 0.6 per cent rise in the consumer price index, it would appear that between 1980 and 1985 the consumer price index would rise by 12 per cent solely as a result of higher fuel costs.

The basic implications of the energy price strategy are ominous for the inflation statistics. Clearly these increases are not part of the normal cyclical pattern and this inflation cannot be regarded as monetary. Also, the increases are not just one-time shifts in relative prices but rather a continuing medium-term structural change. It is also likely, in view of the recent events in OPEC and the Middle East, that Canada will continue to face increases in energy costs for some years.

In the 1970s wage settlements in the Canadian labour market developed structural characteristics that made it almost impossible to moderate wage and salary increases to rates consistent with the price increases of a decade earlier. Even though the economic literature to explain money wage changes in terms of excess labour supply (the unemployment rate) and inflationary expectations is lengthy, in fact there appears to be a lower limit to wage settlements in Canada that is influenced partly by the market power of organized labour, partly by the cross-border wage ties between Canada and the United States, and partly by automatic cost-of-living adjustments to wage payments. The fact that the apparent threshold rate of wage and salary settlements rose in the 1970s even though unemployment increased sharply is one manifestation of the underlying cost push that cannot be easily eradicated from the economy.

Similarly, many service and commodity prices are relatively inflexible, although it is difficult to demonstrate statistically rising market power either in the labour market or the commodity and services market. The "downward inflexibility" of wages has been explored by Professor Sidney Weintraub, who has pointed out that economic theory provides little insight into how money wages are determined in industrial countries.[7] He argues that there is a missing equation in most macroeconomic models that would explain the wage-setting process. The reason for its absence is not because no one has tried to develop an equation but rather because the equation must include sociological and historical variables, which economists are uncomfortable with or do not understand. We share his exasperation and concern.

The essence of what we are arguing is that several rather extraordinary events occurred in the 1970s producing inflationary forces that could not be expected to moderate quickly. The inflationary pressures that emerged from energy price hikes and historically high increases in money wages could not be described as normally cyclical. The energy part of the structural wave of inflation is far from over. Indeed, even as Canada attempts to close the price gap, the world price has moved up. As well, money wage settlements in 1979 are apparently already past the 1978 lower limit of a 6 to 7 per cent annual rate of increase.

Finally, we must note that, with the benefit of hindsight, the effects of the seemingly responsible price strategy Canada pursued on the energy front and the monetary strategy of gradualism may both have been self-defeating. The policy of raising energy prices gradually resulted in increases in structural inflation, while the goal of achieving the world price remains elusive. In addition, the energy price rise did not have the desired immediate effect of rapidly increasing energy supplies or substantially moderating the use of energy in Canada. While the authorities informed Canadians that a monetary policy of economic gradualism would result in only a mild reduction in the rate of inflation, the rate did not moderate and the game plan, in itself, at least partly sustained the high rate of inflation by maintaining inflationary expectations.

Policies to Deal with Structural Inflation

The crux of much of our criticism of the Bank of Canada's position since 1975 is that its policies attempted to deal with severe inflationary pressures as if they were of a monetary origin or were rooted in excess demand. Monetary gradualism, or so-called gradual economic restraint, was doomed to fail in terms of such stubborn structural inflationary forces. In the late 1970s, tight monetary policy was an inappropriate response to inflation. Monetary policy could not, however, possibly have moderated rapid increases in food prices in 1978 and 1979. Nor could monetary policy do much to lower the floor rate of wage and price inflation, which was in turn related to the seemingly high money wage settlements in the recent past. And the rising cost of energy was certainly beyond the control of any central bank.

Canada's policy of seeking self-reliance in energy and its international trade in energy forced the federal government into a policy direction that was very inflationary. But, it is difficult to see how Canada could have developed an energy policy that would have been anti-inflationary. A variant of three energy price strategies was and is still open to Canada's policymakers: keep energy costs stable; allow them to rise slowly to world levels as at present; or bring energy prices immediately to world levels and allow for future increases to keep them equivalent. In a trading nation such as Canada the first option of stable prices implies distortions and subsidies that appear to make that option both impractical and unsustainable. The second option seems doomed to add to domestic inflation in a predictable and worsening manner. The third option of dramatically increasing domestic prices to world price levels would have the immediate impact of increasing inflation and would also bring with it a serious deceleration in economic growth. It would likely, however, reduce the long-run structural inflation. But there would continue to be energy price rises whenever world prices rose unless Canada's inflation were so reduced that a rising exchange rate absorbed the external price hikes.[8] Thus the last two options have little anti-inflation appeal and energy policy, if it wishes to avoid the distortions and subsidies inherent in stable prices, must continue to stress other goals, such as self-reliance.[9]

As well, in the 1980s, the continued downward inflexibility of prices and wages will likely result in an unsatisfactory high floor to the inflation rate even if the economy continues to be progressively weak. Unfortunately, increases in product market concentration associated with the late 1970s corporate merger movement—particularly in the retail industries—may make the economy more inflationary.

45

From a policy perspective, inflation must in the final analysis be contained within the labour market. This is not to say that the labour movement causes inflation; rather, this assertion simply takes note of the dynamic socioeconomic reality that, once high inflation becomes built into money wages in Canada, it becomes very difficult to moderate settlements, and the production and employment costs of fighting inflation rise. Tight money may erode inflation, but it does so in a non-neutral fashion and with a long delay, and slow economic growth and higher unemployment result.

The usual explanation of how tight economic policies—and monetary policies—moderate inflation in a closed economy is as follows: higher interest costs and the lesser availability of credit result, with a delay, in a dampening of private spending, particularly in the interest-sensitive sectors such as housing, capital investment, and consumer durables purchases. The associated reduction in economic growth will force a higher rate of unemployment after some period of time. With a further delay there will be some moderation in inflationary expectations. The feedback effect of lower inflationary expectations and the recession itself will tend to moderate both wages and prices. Firms presumably lose some ability to mark up prices over costs when faced with declining sales, while lower inflationary expectations feed back into presumably lower negotiated money wage settlements.

Tight monetary policies have obviously not had this effect on the economy recently. In addition, the accompanying mandatory incomes policies under the anti-inflation programme designed to either shorten the recession-inflation feedback effect or to attack the structural imbalances in the economy directly have fallen far short of their goals, since they have tended to retard domestic investment in the process and their lasting impact on inflation in both the product and labour markets were limited. For these reasons we suggest that Canada should carefully examine a policy that uses the tax system as a means of curbing the growth of money incomes to rates of increase more consistent with non-inflationary economic growth.

A Tax-Based Incomes Policy

A "tax-based incomes policy" (TIP) would focus on the need to recognize that the market at the microeconomic level does not operate in an efficient manner when faced with recessions designed to reduce inflation. Such a policy, originally proposed by H. Wallich and S. Weintraub, gained wide support in the United States.[10] TIP plans might vary but basically would involve the imposition of a progressive surtax on corporate income, depending upon the degree to which the corporation granted money wage and salary gains in excess of a government-set norm regarded as non-inflationary.

Sidney Weintraub has written extensively on the subject both from the perspective of designing a comprehensive framework for the operation of a tax-based incomes policy as well as explaining the theoretical underpinnings of such a plan.[11] He argues persuasively that a direct policy must be implemented to curb the growth of money incomes without retarding the growth of economic activity. While his proposal is a somewhat radical departure from traditional macroeconomic policies, it follows from his view that money wage behaviour is not linked in any simple manner to macroeconomic variables. Abba P. Lerner supports this view:

> The laws of supply and demand did not work for a general deficiency of demand, but the law of excess demand lost none of its power to cause wages to rise in response to excess demand—that is, to an increase in total spending when there already was full employment. This asymmetry—wage flexibility upward but inflexibility downward—indicates that something was missing in the Keynesian revolution.[12]

To the extent that total wage and salary earnings represent a large part of the cost of doing business, Weintraub's proposal can be labelled a cost-push inflation theory. But the demand-pull element is equally important. The demand for goods and services is derived from available wage and salary incomes. Since wage and salary incomes determine both the aggregate demand and the costs of goods and services, they are the key to halting the inflation process in his analysis. It is Weintraub's view, with which we concur, that what is missing from analytical discussions about inflation is an adequate theory of money wage determination. Tight economic policies retard the growth of money incomes primarily through job losses rather than through restraint of wage and salary increases.

Available research indicates that most firms in North America tend to price on the basis of a markup over their average unit labour costs. The markup changes with the business cycle and economic conditions, but on average does not vary much. Thus, in Weintraub's view, it is the pay variable, as it enters into the firm's price, that is important. An inflationary money wage settlement is passed on to the public very quickly by firms under the markup pricing system.

How would Weintraub's TIP scheme operate, assuming that a 5 per cent average pay norm is adopted as a policy target?

- Firms would compute their average wage and salary rates of increase in a particular year. For example, if in 1979 wage and salary increases were in excess of the 5 per cent norm for a particular firm, that firm would be subject to an extra corporation income tax. Production workers could, in principle, derive a greater than 5 per cent average increase if other employees took less. Alternatively, a settlement larger than 5 per cent may be justified by economic conditions, and firms would be willing to pay the extra tax.
- To encourage productivity improvements, some part of an exceptional productivity gain could be shared with the particular firm's labour force.
- Weintraub proposed to apply the TIP plan to the 1,000 largest employing companies in the United States. In Canada an appropriate number might be 200. In Weintraub's view, the extra administration costs to government of overseeing a TIP plan would be slight.
- The TIP policy is not designed to earn extra tax revenues. Indeed, if extra tax revenues were raised because of TIP, the corporation tax rate could be reduced so as to maintain a fairly uniform level of tax collections.
- As a supplement to the proposal, Professor Weintraub argued that the effects of TIP could be augmented by another plan. On all government construction contracts, or government-assisted contracts, a clause could be inserted requiring that over the life of the contract the average pay for wage earners and executives be limited to the pay target norm. This policy, which is described as a contract authorization incomes policy (CAIP), would use the direct influence of government, as a major purchaser of labour time, to moderate costs.

In the Canadian setting a TIP plan would have to be augmented to take into account public sector wages and salaries and the federal-provincial reality. Thus for a scheme such as TIP to have any success, some additional considerations must also be worked out carefully. TIP must be regarded as part of a package of proposals to promote fuller levels of employment and lower rates of price inflation. Without policies to stimulate job creation, the TIP approach would quickly lose credibility, since it would appear to be anti-labour.

There has not been a comprehensive programme that attacked inflation directly from a tax-incentive basis. A modified TIP proposal

48

should be carefully examined by Canada's policymakers. Such a proposal, although untried, is widely discussed in the economic literature and should not have adverse real effects on the economy. Unlike other incomes policies it has the advantage of not being discredited. A Canadian TIP programme might include the following elements:

- a wage and salary norm and increases in corporation taxes when the norm was exceeded;
- an appropriate shift in Ottawa's current macroeconomic policies towards a posture designed to expand output and employment;
- agreements that federal and provincial public employees be bound by identical wage and salary guidelines;
- wage and salary guidelines for contracts let by all levels of government, particularly contracting to the construction trade.
- a federal government commitment to the public that the augmented TIP plan would be administered fairly. If it could be determined that real wages or purchasing power were being curtailed unfairly, or that TIP were providing excess profits, then further tax measures would be introduced to remedy the situation.[13]

In summary, the basic policy tool that should be considered to complement demand-management policies is a form of tax-based incomes policy in association with wage and salary guidelines for the public sector. The effective ceiling on wage and salary rate of increases in the private sector (which would trigger higher corporation tax rates if exceeded) would have to be the ceiling rate in the public sector. These policies would have to be worked out in collaboration with the provinces to set provincial public service wage settlement ceilings and to consider the revenue sharing effects.

The TIP scheme would have no effect on the energy or food factors in Canada's inflation. It would, however, provide an additional tool to temper wage and salary settlements; to the extent that they influence the structural aspects of inflation it could have some impact on reducing inflation.[14] In essence, it could add to the effectiveness of macroeconomic policies, making further job creation possible in a less inflationary environment.

Conclusion
This chapter has stressed that a good part of the high inflation experienced after 1975 could not be regarded as normally cyclical in that it

was not responsive to weaker aggregate demand conditions associated with tight economic policies. Moreover, the linkage between a given level of wage and salary inflation, energy inflation, and monetary policy became very remote in the second-half of the 1970s. Unfortunately structural inflation is not a transitory phenomenon. In addition, the expected tripling of domestic fuel costs over the next five years will add heavily to increased inflation.

It is clear that policymakers will require an additional instrument to deal with the wave of structural inflation. One is drawn immediately to some form of an incomes policy, but such policies have been badly discredited in North America. Indeed, a real challenge for policymakers is to design an incomes policy that is effective, administratively efficient, and reasonably equitable.

We argue that a modified form of the original Wallich-Weintraub TIP plan could achieve these multiple objectives and, at the same time, provide only minimal disincentives to business and labour. The TIP plan would be administratively efficient and would provide a potential extra corporate tax liability if large private corporations granted wage and salary increases in excess of a norm established for the public sector.

While wages and salaries are the variable directly affected in this plan, a successful programme should, in principle, not harm the real purchasing power of labour if the plan is successful in moderating inflation. To ensure that the latter is the case, the federal government could commit itself to additional tax cuts for low- and middle-income wage earners in the event that price inflation is regarded as too steep relative to money wage and salary gains.

Domestic Concerns for the Future

5

This chapter focuses on some macroeconomic concerns for the Canadian economy in the medium-term. To this end, a series of medium-term projections is reviewed in order to consider the likely impact of the projected rates of economic growth, inflation, employment, and capital investment on economic policy.

The projections set out in Table 5-1, with the exception of those of the Department of Finance, all indicate that Canada's economic outlook for the next five years is not very promising. Demographic shifts in the 1980s will lead to slower labour force growth as well as a more moderate full-capacity rate of growth of the economy. Obviously these projections foreshadow potential policy problems, some of which are the result of problems not satisfactorily resolved in the 1970s. For example, the unemployment-inflation dilemma will likely continue to plague the Canadian economy in the 1980s as it did in the 1970s.

The Economic Council of Canada, in its *Fifteenth Annual Review* projects in its "pre-austerity" solution that real GNP growth will average over 4 per cent in 1980 and 1981 but will then decline sharply. Business investment will remain strong until 1981 and then fall off rather sharply as well. Price inflation is projected to average about 7 per cent until 1983, and the national unemployment rate to move to only slightly below 8 per cent in the early 1980s. These projections assume that the economic policy framework that existed in 1978 will be extended until 1983. In the same Review, the Council also set out a series of ten other alternative macroeconomic scenarios, all of which are rather gloomy:

> If governments maintain their commitment to keep public spending below the growth rate of GNE—or even if they hold it to a level roughly equal

TABLE 5-1
AVERAGE ANNUAL GROWTH RATE OF SELECTED ECONOMIC INDICATORS IN THE MEDIUM TERM, VARIOUS FORECASTS

	Real GNP	Nominal GNP	GNP deflator	Consumer price index	Labour force	Employment	Unemployment rate	Average Wages
			PRICES			LABOUR		
			(Per cent)					
Economic Council of Canada, Twelfth Annual Review								
1975-80	5.7	12.2	7.1	7.0				
1980-85	3.6	9.8	5.9	5.2				
1975-85	4.6	11.0	6.1	6.2				
Economic Council of Canada, Fourteenth Annual Review								
1977-82	4.3			7.1			8.2	
Economic Council of Canada, Fifteenth Annual Review								
1979	4.2		7.2				8.3	
1980	3.9		7.6				8.0	
1981	4.6		6.8				7.5	
1982	2.8		7.3				7.6	
1983	3.0		6.6				7.6	

Ontario Economic Council,					
1978-82	5.0	9.9	4.7	2.4	
Department of Industry,					
Trade and Commerce					
1975-85	3.9	6.6	2.56		
1970-85				2.19	5.8
					(in 1985)
Department of Finance					
1978-81	5.5		4.7	2.2	2.8	6.8

Source: Economic Council of Canada, *Twelfth Annual Review: Options for Growth* (Ottawa: Information Canada, 1974), pp. 146-47; *Fourteenth Annual Review: Into the 1980s* (Ottawa: Supply and Services Canada, 1978) *Fifteenth Annual Review: A Time for Reason* (Ottawa: Supply and Services Canada, 1978); D. Foot, *Et.al, The Ontario Economy, 1977-1987* (Toronto: Ontario Economic Council, 1977); Department of Industry, Trade and Commerce, *Simulation Experiments of the Effect of the Tokyo Round* (Ottawa, 1977), Appendix C, p. 10. Department of Finance, *Canada's Economy: Medium-Term Projections and Targets* (Ottawa, 1978), p. 64.

to the growth rate of GNE, and there is no startling resurgence of domestic and foreign demand—Canadians can expect to live with persistently high unemployment rates for quite a few years yet. A corollary is that without the type of fortuitous and unforeseen developments described in several of the simulations, it is most unlikely that the Canadian economy can reach and sustain a 5 per cent real annual growth rate in GNE in the next few years. If all governments adhere to an austere fiscal stance, and this is combined with tight monetary policy at the Bank of Canada, the medium-term real growth prospects beyond 1981 fall dismally to levels in the 2 per cent range. Unemployment rates rise to almost double-digit levels, with the only bright spot being the reduced government and current account deficits as a percentage of GNE. Inflation, as measured by the GNE deflator, will continue at annual rates of between 6 and 8 per cent.[1]

The Department of Finance projection is concerned more with how an economic recovery could occur in the late 1970s and early 1980s than whether it will occur. An important part of that recovery scenario is the continuation of the projected slowdown in money wages and unit labour costs that would boost corporate profits. The Department of Finance also expected fairly rapid growth in non-residential business investment and exports to lead the recovery.

The Unemployment Issue

The outlook for the early to mid-1980s is rather dismal, too, for Canada's unemployment problem. In early 1979 the economy was faced with a high unemployment rate, and it was widely recognized that comfortable levels of unemployment could only be achieved over a fairly long period.

The explanation of Canada's poor unemployment rate in the second-half of the 1970s was directly related to slow economic growth. Since the end of 1973 the economy has grown an average of about 3 per cent a year, while labour productivity increased about 1.0 per cent. Both these measures of economic progress are low by historical standards. The real economic growth rate between 1955 and 1973 averaged about 6 per cent annually, while labour productivity advanced 2 per cent. As a result, in the 1970s the growth in labour demand, which in turn stems from the growth in GNP, fell by about one-half from its earlier pace.

Labour productivity improvements have also been below average since 1973. Nevertheless, even the 1.0 per cent productivity growth figure means that every year output must increase by 1.0 per cent simply

54

to employ a constant number of workers. Moreover, the work force has increased at the record rate since 1973 of 3.5 per cent a year, indicating that employment and output must rise by at least that rate to maintain a constant unemployment rate.

Bringing these trends together—productivity improvements that create unemployment unless offset by additional demand, and the increase in the labour force—one observes that the economy would have had to advance in real terms at about a 4.5 per cent annual rate since 1973 just to maintain a constant unemployment rate. If labour productivity had been more typical of Canada's experience, the required real growth rate would have been in the range of 5.5 per cent annually. Thus it is not surprising that the unemployment rate rose from a 5.5 per cent level in 1972 to a high of 8.5 per cent by mid-1978, though it declined to below 8 per cent in 1979.

Large numbers of unemployed are distressing not only because of the personal anguish and the production and standard of living losses that result, but also because it may take a very long time to reduce the numbers of unemployed, partly because of employment lags when rapid economic growth begins. Indeed, if the full-capacity real annual growth rate were approximately 5.5 per cent, with no changes in productivity or labour force growth rates, a one percentage point increase in real economic growth to 6.5 per cent could reduce the national unemployment rate by about 1 per cent. In other words, one full calendar year of exceptionally strong economic activity is required to reduce the unemployment rate by one percentage point. Yet most of the medium-term forecasts project only modest real economic growth rates into the early 1980s.

More optimistically, if the Department of Finance projections for output, labour force, and productivity trends emerged, then the unemployment rate could decline by approximately 0.7 percentage points per year. But even with this fairly rosy picture, the unemployment rate would only decline from 8.5 per cent in 1978 to about 6.7 per cent by 1982.

Using the recent past as a guide to future economic performance suggests that the present high unemployment rate could well persist until the early 1980s unless policies are designed deliberately to generate faster than capacity economic growth rates. If such a strategy included the elimination of the 1979 projected $7 billion dollar current account deficit, that factor alone could reduce Canada's unemployment rate by as much as 2 percentage points.[2]

Inflation in the 1980s and Objectives for Policymakers

Inflation will likely remain at unusually high levels in the 1980s. The Economic Council of Canada in its *Fifteenth Review* projected a 7.1 per cent average annual rate of increase of prices between 1979 and 1983, a pace of inflation that appears at the low end of a realistic range considering the future energy price adjustment the economy must make. But perhaps the most significant inflation forecast is embodied in the capital market yield curves and their implicit forecast. In mid-1979 long-term government of Canada bonds were yielding about 10 per cent, while real rates of return to such investments are thought to be about 2.5 to 3 per cent. These markets are betting on a Canadian average annual rate of inflation over the next ten to twenty years of above 7 per cent a year.

In view of the pessimistic inflation projections, what policies or objectives should the economic authorities in Canada pursue? Is it sufficient to attempt to contain Canada's inflation to a level no higher than that in the United States? Or should Canada attempt to generate even lower rates of inflation than are present in the United States?

Some industrial nations, such as Germany, Switzerland, and Japan, have been very successful in containing inflation since 1977, despite their heavy dependence on fuel imports. But, of course, the western European countries moved immediately to world energy prices as they saw they had no choice, offset the negative effect on their economy by repatriating foreign labour, and had moderate labour market settlements even after energy prices rose. The Japanese case was a bit different, although there was also no choice other than to accept world energy price levels. Still Japan has apparently absorbed the economic impact successfully. In both Germany and Japan, export growth sustained their economies and, aided by a general fear of world inflation, their currencies have appreciated against North America's since 1973. In effect, their currency moves were in the right direction to limit the inflationary effect of higher energy costs.

It is obvious that Canada in the 1980s will face some difficult policy decisions about inflation and economic growth, but it should be recognized that slow growth by itself in the 1980s is unlikely to deliver a substantially lower inflation rate. Indeed, this should be one of the lessons learned from the monetarist and anti-inflation experiment in the 1970s. This should not mean that policymakers give up on inflation, but rather that new policies to alter structural problems—particularly those designed to moderate the growth in money incomes—must be developed to bring inflation down to an acceptable level. In the longer term, Canada should aim for a lower rate of inflation such as that achieved in the 1950s and the 1960s.

The Savings-Investment Scenario

Another major policy concern is whether Canada can generate sufficient savings in the 1980s to finance its heavy capital investment needs. Tables 5-2 to 5-4 set out a variety of medium-term savings, investment, and energy scenarios for Canada, drawing from several different studies. All the studies project a rise in the share of energy capital to both total capital formation and GNP. In the main, these medium-term projections see moderating growth in residential capital formation and increasing energy investment growth during the 1980s.[3] Many officials and private individuals view these heavy investment demands with some trepidation, wondering whether such financing will adversely affect the dollar and hence the economy.

But one must keep such investment forecasts in their proper perspective. While they appear to imply huge energy and other investment expenditures, there is no reason why these requirements cannot be financed out of domestic savings. Indeed, with the housing and social capital requirements declining as a proportion of GNP because of demographic factors, there should be sufficient domestic savings available to finance the growing projected energy capital requirements.

TABLE 5-2
CANADIAN CAPITAL EXPENDITURES, 1967-90

	Housing	Social	Energy	Other industrial	Total	Capital as a proportion of GNE
	(Billions of current dollars)					
1967	2.8	3.0	2.1	7.8	15.7	25.4
1978	13.3	7.5	10.2	21.7	52.7	22.7
1984	19.7	12.3	26.1	43.5	101.6	23.4
1990	29.2	19.8	54.2	90.2	193.4	25.8
	(Annual percentage increase)					
1967-78	15.2	8.7	15.5	9.7	11.6	
1979-84	7.2	8.7	17.0	12.5	11.9	
1984-90	6.8	8.3	13.0	12.9	11.3	

Source: Department of Economic Research, Toronto-Dominion Bank, *Business and Economics*, Vol. 8, No. 1 (March 1979), p. 12.

TABLE 5-3
ANNUAL INCREASE IN CANADIAN REAL INVESTMENT, 1965-87

	Growth in real investment
	(Annual percentage increase)
1965–70	3.28
1970–75	5.82
1975–77	1.48
1977–82	7.51
1982–87	2.43

Source: D. K. Foot, *et al.*, *The Ontario Economy, 1977-1987* (Toronto: Ontario Economic Council, 1977) p. 77.

TABLE 5-4
CANADIAN ENERGY INVESTMENT, 1976-90

	Total investment in energy	Energy investment as a proportion of GNP
	(Billions of 1975 dollars)	(Per cent)
1976–80	45.7	5.0
1981–85	75.1	6.5
1986–90	60.2	4.2
1976–90	181.0	5.2

Source: Department of Energy, Mines and Resources, Canada, *An Energy Strategy for Canada* (Ottawa: Information Canada, 1977).

These expanded capital investment requirements need not force the abandonment of the balanced current account goal.

Conclusion

In summary, a review of the macroeconomic prospects for the 1980s suggests that the problems of the coming decade may be very similar to those of the 1970s. As noted elsewhere in this study, the policy of energy self-reliance unfortunately will lead to severe structural inflation. In addition, the probable moderation of the growth rate of the labour force in the 1980s does not carry with it an obvious solution to the unemployment problem unless Canada is able to eliminate its high

58

international current account deficit. If serious attention is not given to the introduction of measures for generating less inflationary but more rapid rates of domestic growth, the economy may simply face a repetition of the economic difficulties of the 1970s. Clearly the structural forces that were discussed in the previous chapter will dominate the price movements in the early to mid-1980s just as they have in the past decade. A key ingredient in reaching a solution to the growth, employment, and inflation problems of the 1980s is the large current account deficit in the balance of payments. That issue is singled out for discussion in the following chapter.

Monetary Policy and the Balance of Payments Problem

Any comment on Canadian economic policy must take into account the fact that Canada operates in, and is very much influenced by, the world environment. It must also be recognized that the international sector of the economy should serve the needs of Canadian output, employment, and incomes as much as possible. Perhaps the continuing crucial element in the economy is the external value of the dollar, which affects major changes in the levels of incomes, output, and employment. Clearly, government policymakers must be aware of this. The exchange rate is affected by both domestic policies and factors external to and not controllable from within Canadian borders. Thus the subject of the interaction of monetary policy with the balance of payments is difficult and complex.

Recent Balance of Payments Problems

As the Canadian dollar declined steadily through 1978, the federal government announced both new borrowings and new bond issues, the proceeds of which were to be used to replenish exchange reserves to support the faltering external value of the Canadian dollar. The federal authorities described their actions as "smoothing operations," necessary to ensure "orderly markets in foreign exchange," but it was evident that they felt obliged to finance the massive current account deficit in international transactions. The obvious anomaly of these borrowings was that they were used to support a weakening dollar when the cause of that weakness was too much borrowing in foreign markets over the previous four years (see Table 3-3). The serious exchange rate crisis in September 1978 was clearly related to the monetary and other policies followed in prior years. The problem for 1979 and beyond is how to move away from these entanglements of the 1970s onto a more secure, stable, and strong economic growth path in the 1980s. A necessary corollary is the question of how to achieve a viable international payments position.

The fact is that Canada is caught in a spiral of rising external debt and interest payments abroad causing further debt and is almost incapable of catching up to these increasing payments with new sales of merchandise abroad. The international borrowings of the provincial and federal governments, corporations, and municipalities produced an outflow of interest payments in excess of $3 billion in 1978 (Table 6-1). In 1979 that figure will be closer to $4 billion and in 1980, unless a major adjustment takes place, it could be over $5 billion. As well, Canada must allow for other major service sector payments, such as dividends and the traditional deficit on tourist trade. The total of these items, together with minor accounts, amounts to a balance of payments service account deficit of almost $9 billion for 1978 and an outlook for close to a $10 billion shortfall in 1979. To produce a balanced current account without relying on borrowed foreign capital, Canada must accumulate a very large merchandise trade surplus.[1]

During 1978, however, when the largest merchandise trade surplus ever was amassed by exporting goods of a total value of $52.4 billion while importing goods of a value of $48.9 billion, the current account deficit still totalled about $5.3 billion, and the prospects for 1979 are for a current account deficit of about $7 billion.

Obviously, the major distortion in Canada's balance of international payments stems from the services sector or the trade in invisibles. This includes payments for services to other nations including freight, insurance, banking, and communications services. It also includes tourist expenditures and, most important, the cost of the services of capital; that is, interest and dividend payments. To lower the deficit in the services account, policy could stress the use of domestic freight carriers, insurance, financial services, and communications services. Policies to promote tourist attractions for both Canadians and foreigners would also reduce the traditional deficit on tourist transactions. But even if all these policies were major successes, Canada would be left with payments for the services of capital that cause a huge annual outflow of interest and dividends. The only reasonable way to reduce these payments is to realize a substantial current account surplus that would allow either the repayment of the borrowed debt capital or the export of capital on which interest and dividends would accrue to Canada. Such a current account realignment can only be achieved by major increases in exports of goods and services or the replacement of imported goods and services by those of domestic origin.

61

TABLE 6-1
CANADA'S BALANCE OF PAYMENTS, SELECTED ITEMS, 1974-78

	1974	1975	1976	1977	1978
	($ Millions)				
Merchandise exports	32591	33511	38132	44628	52390
Service receipts	6401	6941	7553	8088	9523
Interest[a]			301	266	222
Dividends[a]	882	926	524	554	831
Travel expenditures	1694	1815	1930	2025	2364
Merchandise imports	30902	33962	36793	41712	48922
Service payments	10107	11627	13204	15520	18252
Interest			1867	2723	3422
Dividends	2435	2879	1430	1577	1936
Travel expenditures	1978	2542	3121	3666	4083
	(Percentage of GNP)				
Interest and dividend[a] payments	1.7	1.7	1.7	2.1	2.3
Interest payments			1.0	1.3	1.5
Dividend payments			0.7	0.8	0.8
	($ Millions)				
Long-term capital Canadian securities					
New issues	2423	5038	8986	5936	6560
Retirements	− 626	− 851	− 933	− 938	− 1115
Net new issues	1797	4187	8053	4998	5445

[a] Separate figures for interest and dividends are only available for last three years.

Note: A negative amount (−) indicates an outflow of capital from Canada and represents an increase in holdings of assets abroad or a reduction in liabilities to nonresidents.

Source: Statistics Canada, *Quarterly Estimates of the Canadian Balance of International Payments*, Cat. 67-001, fourth quarter, 1978.

The expansion of Canadian production of both import-competing industries and of our major exporters is essential for the 1980s. This means that goods must be competitively produced, and domestic costs must be kept below foreign costs. But it will take some years to accomplish the necessary industrial shift and to expand production to change the merchandise trade balance significantly. A key ingredient in promoting that shift will be a stable outlook for the external value of the Canadian dollar. Thus an important medium-term development goal must be to promote relative stability in the value of the Canadian dollar, especially in its relation to the U.S. dollar. In addition, the Canadian dollar should not be allowed to rise above a certain level— say, U.S. $0.90—until the high current account deficits have vanished. The reason for concentrating on balancing the current account is that that account—technically, the balance of trade in goods and services— registers the direct foreign trade impact on GNP. A large current account deficit means that Canadian demand is not matched by employment and production in Canada.

Balance of Payments Goals

In considering Canada's economic future, policymakers must decide whether the nation should have goals for its balance of payments or whether such goals should be ignored. In the past, Canada was often fortunate in being rescued from balance of payments problems by a series of new resource developments or greater export markets. But there were no balance of payments goals over the past five years and no rescue prospects are now in sight. The similar U.S. policy of having no balance of payments objectives was called "benign neglect"; the Canadian version might be labelled "malignant neglect," since this policy resulted in large deficits, massive increases in borrowings, and future costs that will have to be paid to restore balance in the external accounts.

But if the present lack of balance of payments goals is not acceptable, then how should policies in Canada change? Should Canada adopt the strategy of a developing country that encourages imports of capital for the development of its industries? Should Canada consider itself a fully developed industrial country and design policies to export capital and in this way allow the developing nations to use its expertise in their development? Or is there some middle position?

The developing country strategy, which encourages a nation to have a major current account deficit financed by imports of capital, is the model followed over the past five years. But instead of using the inflow of capital to produce major industrial projects that would ensure the production of export earnings, Canada in large part financed the expansion of personal consumption of foreign goods rather than capital investment. Indeed, it is very difficult to argue that Canada had a lack of domestic savings, when it had a rising unemployment rate that reached 8.5 per cent in 1978—a reflection of the underutilization of resources and an indication that surpluses could be used for capital projects. Stated another way, there were potentially larger pools of savings available than were required during the late 1970s. If further evidence were needed, the capacity utilization rates of most industries were at their lowest levels ever in late 1977 and early 1978. Thus the developing nation strategy as a guide for designing balance of payments goals must be discarded.

Should Canada then become an exporter of capital to developed or developing nations? It is quite possible to argue that Canada is indeed one of the wealthier nations in the world and that it does not devote a sufficient percentage of its gross national product to helping developing countries. The remote prospect, however, of Canada achieving a substantial current account surplus in the near future seems to put the goal of becoming a capital exporting nation beyond our present reach.

Policymakers in Canada are then left to devise some median strategy. Our answer to the dilemma is that Canada accept as a medium-term goal the achievement of a rough balance on current account—or, more specifically, the balance of trade in goods and services. It seems reasonable to suggest that international economic influences should be neutral over the medium term in their impact on output and employment in the domestic economy. There will, of course, be times when the economy is fully employed and at that time Canadians may wish to import more goods and services from abroad and thus place the current account in deficit. There may also be times when production is under-employed, and Canadians may wish to export more to the international economies because those other economies are fully employed; at such times the current account will be in surplus. But the overall objective should be to achieve a relatively balanced current account in the medium term.

Such a goal will clearly require some restructuring of Canadian industry over the next few years to redress the disastrous performance of the recent past. But the restructuring could be relatively painless in that it implies greater domestic production and employment and a more efficient use of existing resources. It also requires that monetary policy and other government policies be directed specifically towards

64

the rapid achievement of the balance of payments goal. Such policies would be in sharp contrast to monetary policy after 1975 that was dominated by attempts to reach money supply targets and to finance current account deficits.

Provincial Governments and the Balance of Payments

The current account deficits of the recent past have as their mirror image the capital account surpluses. These surpluses on capital account were the result of foreign borrowing, largely by the provinces and their agencies.

In 1975, 1976, and 1977 provincial governments, municipalities, and corporations raised almost $20 billion in foreign capital markets, 60 per cent of which was borrowed by the provinces and their agencies alone. These large-scale borrowings were encouraged by the federal authorities and by a monetary policy that held domestic interest rates substantially above the levels in the United States and other countries. The result was a huge influx of foreign capital, which helped to push the value of the Canadian dollar to unrealistically high levels, particularly in 1976, and made Canadian exports uncompetitive (Table 6-2). At

TABLE 6-2
NET NEW BOND ISSUES OF CANADIAN GOVERNMENTS AND CORPORATIONS, 1973-78

	1973	1975	1976	1977	1978
	($ Billions)				
Government of Canada					
Canadian dollars	−0.6	3.4	2.6	5.5	5.1
Other currencies	−0.1	−	−	−	2.3
Provincial direct and guaranteed					
Canadian dollars	2.1	3.9	4.6	4.2	4.6
Other currencies	0.5	2.9	4.4	2.6	1.8
Municipalities					
Canadian dollars	0.4	0.6	0.5	0.9	0.7
Other currencies	−	0.5	0.7	0.3	−
Corporations					
Canadian dollars	1.6	2.2	1.0	2.7	2.8
Other currencies	−	0.6	2.9	2.1	1.6

Source: *Bank of Canada Review* (January 1979), Tables 31, 32, and 33.

issue here is the question whether provincial borrowing should be allowed to influence the level of Canada's exchange rate in such an adverse manner.

Provinces, municipalities, and corporations borrow abroad, largely in the United States, for several reasons. The first is usually that they need funds to cover provincial deficits, as during the 1975-77 period. Second, provinces and corporations borrow abroad when there is a significant interest rate advantage to do so. In those three years there was a great advantage, largely as a result of Canadian monetary policy. Third, because some provinces and particularly some provincial agencies are very large borrowers, it is often easier to sell a large provincial bond issue in a large market, such as New York, rather than in the smaller market in Canada.

Other measures have been used which in effect counter provincial and municipal borrowings in foreign markets and encourage domestic placement of these governments' issues. For example, provinces have special borrowing rights with the Canada Pension Plan and indeed take advantage of them to the maximum extent possible because of their preferred interest rate. Further, a withholding tax on interest and dividends paid abroad imposed by the federal government acts as a penalty to the Canadian borrower for borrowing in a foreign market or as an instrument for the Canadian government to tax the incomes earned in Canada by non-residents. It is also a device that insulates Canadian capital markets from those abroad and allows monetary policy a further degree of freedom.[2]

The other method of separating Canadian and foreign capital markets is by guideline or moral suasion. In 1970 the federal government introduced foreign borrowing guidelines that requested "Canadian borrowers to explore fully the Canadian capital market before floating issues abroad."[3] In February 1975 these guidelines were withdrawn by the Minister of Finance, who announced that "the government no longer wishes Canadian borrowers to feel constrained by the request." He also exempted the provincial governments from the withholding tax on interest for three years.[4] Later, in a budget, the withholding tax on longer term corporate borrowings was removed.

These two events—the withdrawal of foreign borrowing guidelines and the elimination of withholding taxes in the mid-1970s—allowed provinces and corporations to borrow large sums abroad between 1976 and 1978. Indeed, it was clearly the intent of the federal government to encourage such borrowing. While the stated purpose for removing the withholding tax was to allow Canadian corporations to borrow more

66

cheaply abroad, the result was to place Canadian business, especially cost competitive manufacturing industries, at a disadvantage in both domestic and foreign markets, since unnecessarily high capital inflows after 1975 led to an unrealistically high external value of the Canadian dollar.

These three measures—the setting of deliberately high interest rates; the elimination of the withholding tax; and the policy of encouraging provinces to borrow in foreign capital markets by the removal of the guidelines—demonstrated the intention of the federal authorities to raise the external value of the Canadian dollar in 1976. The government could have offset borrowing by purchasing an equivalent amount of U.S. dollars, thereby preventing provincial, municipal, and corporate foreign commitments from affecting the exchange rate.[5]

It is worth while considering the mechanics of the transaction when the federal government deliberately offsets the exchange rate impact of foreign borrowing in order to understand the effects on the domestic economy. For example, when a province borrows U.S. $100 million and sells those dollars on the exchange market, the Canadian government would purchase the U.S. $100 million on the exchange market and place that amount in exchange reserves that are usually invested in U.S. government securities. The Canadian government then must borrow an equivalent amount of Canadian dollars, through an issue of debt securities, for example, or through a larger issue of Canada Savings Bonds. Looked at in this way, the federal government borrows domestic dollars from Canadians and lends them to the provinces through the intermediation of the foreign capital market. *This seems a rather unnecessary, indirect, and expensive exercise* for the Canadian people to finance provincial debt through foreign capital markets.

Of course, in periods of high interest rates in Canada the provinces are able to borrow more cheaply abroad. Then with the federal government paying a much higher rate of interest on its Canadian borrowings it in effect subsidizes the borrowing costs of the provinces. When Canadian interest rates are high and U.S. or other foreign rates are low, there is a substantial advantage for every province to try and get its share of borrowing in international markets and earn its transfers of "subsidized interest" from the federal government. In such a case foreigners make substantial interest gains at the expense of Canadians, because Canada is paid interest at U.S. Treasury security rates and Canadians pay interest abroad at the substantially higher rate paid by provinces and their agencies.

There may also be a circular effect in operation in that the purchase of exchange reserves leads the federal government to borrow in Canada, forcing Canadian interest rates higher and encouraging Canadians to borrow abroad, which causes further capital inflows. Such an effect would likely be minor unless the Canadian economy were fully employed and thus short of savings. In an underemployed economy the effect should be small, as domestic savings are more than adequate. But even the minor effect could be offset by a withholding tax on interest payments that would tend to separate Canadian from foreign capital markets.

There may, of course, be another reason for encouraging provinces, municipalities, and corporations to borrow abroad. For instance, if Canada needs the foreign exchange because the current account is in deficit, then foreign borrowings may be needed to balance that account. But if that were the case, perhaps it would be more appropriate for the federal government to issue the foreign debt. After all, its credit is surely superior to that of the provincial governments or the municipalities or the corporations, and its borrowing costs, which are reflected in the cost to the public, should be much lower than those of any other borrowers. If the cost to the public is to be minimized, then the federal government should borrow abroad, not the provinces, municipalities, and corporations.

How should Ottawa respond if in the future there were to be large-scale borrowings by the provincial governments and their agencies or corporations that again seemed likely to force the Canadian dollar up to an unacceptably high level? In the event, the federal government would face two unacceptable alternatives.

The first alternative would be to offset the foreign exchange effects of massive provincial government borrowings; that is, purchase the U.S. dollars borrowed and place them in the exchange fund. If the government followed that course, it would be investing in U.S. Treasury securities at substantially lower yields than the provincial governments would be paying on their securities, and there would be a net interest loss to Canada from such intermediation. The federal government would also have to borrow Canadian funds to purchase those U.S. dollars and would thus be subsidizing the provinces that borrowed abroad; provinces that did not borrow abroad would not receive the federal subsidy. The New York or European capital markets assume the risk of lending to the individual Canadian provinces, but they do so for a substantial fee. It does not seem reasonable that the people of Canada would want to pay an additional cost to the international capital markets in order for the government of Canada to borrow

Canadian funds at home and relend these funds through these intermediaries to the provincial governments.[6]

The second alternative would be for the federal government not to
offset the borrowings of the provincial governments in international
capital markets. In this case, large borrowings by the provinces would,
with a delay, affect the level of the current account balance, throwing it
into deficit to offset the surplus on capital account by means of a
sharply appreciating Canadian exchange rate. Such reactions would not
occur in an organized fashion but rather under conditions affecting the
demand and supply of Canadian currency in international foreign exchange markets.

Perhaps the effects can be seen more clearly by following the adjustment process through domestic savings. When there are massive capital
inflows the external value of the domestic currency rises, encouraging
imports and discouraging exports. Domestic economic activity weakens,
reducing employment and incomes. As a result of the decline in income, savings fall to a lower equilibrium level. When domestic savings
are replaced by foreign savings, the result must be a lower level of
income and employment unless an offsetting rise in investment occurs.
But an overvalued exchange rate discourages investment when the
exchange rate is expected to remain high. High exchange rates also
restrict profits, reducing corporate saving and the funds available for
investment.

The effect of the exchange rate on investment decisions was clearly
negative in Canada in the mid-1970s. If the Canadian dollar had been
seen as temporarily too high, such would not necessarily have been the
case. Business investors at that time saw the Canadian dollar as stable
but also perceived that costs were rising more rapidly in Canada than
in the United States. Their investment decisions in many cases related
to plant location or expansion in Ontario as opposed to Ohio, for
example, and they did not allow in their decisions for the possible
future devaluation of the Canadian dollar and the accompanying reduction in Canadian plant costs to below those of U.S. plants.[7] Such a
position is quite understandable given the difficulty and inaccuracy of
forecasting foreign exchange rates.

The winner in terms of jobs and production in this set of circumstances is the foreign country that experiences increased demand, production, and employment because of the overvalued Canadian currency. While changes in the terms of trade are a separate issue, they
would tend to increase purchasing power in foreign markets when
employment at home is falling. The loser is Canada, for it has lost

employment and production that can never be recouped despite some marginal gains that may be obtained from improved terms of trade.

Thus we argue that it does not seem reasonable that the provincial governments should be allowed to affect employment and output through the Canadian exchange rate because of unco-ordinated operations in the foreign exchange markets. The conclusion is, therefore, that neither alternative is acceptable and that some other course must be found.

There is also a theoretical point that should be mentioned here. Professor Richard Lipsey of Queen's University argues that the inflow of capital—that is, the borrowing by the provinces, municipalities, and corporations—determines the extent of the deficit on current account and not vice versa.[8] If high interest rate policies are pursued in Canada and this causes provinces, municipalities, and corporations to borrow abroad, then government policy is effectively forcing Canada's current account into deficit to offset these capital inflows. Conversely, if Ottawa desires a relatively balanced current account, then it must establish a policy that discourages provinces, municipalities, and corporations from borrowing abroad since excessive borrowing could force the current account into a deficit position.

Essentially, then, there are three possible explanations of the interaction between the current and capital accounts in the balance of payments. The first is that the current account balance determines the need for capital and the capital funds are then forthcoming. The second is that the capital account determines the level of the current account. The third and eclectic view is that the capital and current account are simultaneously determined. The last explanation is possibly the most reasonable, but when the items making up the current and capital accounts are considered carefully, it is striking that the most exogenous, independent items are found in the capital account. This is especially true of government borrowings that could as a matter of deliberate policy be issued domestically or in foreign markets.[9]

Canadian policymakers should consider possible methods of restraining foreign borrowing unless it is in the domestic interest. Policies to retain provincial, municipal, and corporate borrowing in domestic markets might include the imposition of a sizable withholding tax on the payment of all interest on foreign borrowings. Such policies might also include borrowing abroad by the federal government to offset a current account deficit and the repayment of those borrowings to offset a current account surplus.[10] By accepting the goal of a relative balance on the current account for the medium term, and its associated goal of a relative balance in the capital account, federal borrowings abroad would be increased in periods of current account deficit and repaid in periods of current account surplus with no net federal borrowings abroad in the medium term.

These goals may not be possible in the short term, but are reasonable and attainable in the medium term—say, by the mid-1980s. We recognize that these measures, which have as an ultimate objective a balanced current account, are inconsistent with the monetarist notion of freely fluctuating exchange rates. But then so is any policy mix that attempts to manage the exchange rate.

If the provinces are discouraged or prevented from borrowing in international markets, what could be done to improve their financial access to Canadian markets? Capital markets in Canada would function better if they were broadened and deepened, which would be the case if more provincial, municipal, and corporate borrowing occurred within Canada. This was clearly one result of the 1970 guidelines that successfully switched major amounts of such borrowing from international to Canadian capital markets.[11]

The federal government should consider using incentives to promote this goal as well as legislation that imposes penalties on borrowing abroad. The incentives could include a federal guarantee of a limited amount of provincial bonds, provided the provinces agreed not to borrow in external markets. This would lower the costs of provincial borrowing in Canada since the provincial securities would now carry the federal status. The penalties could include the imposition of a withholding tax on the payment of all interest abroad, whether by provincial or municipal governments or corporations. Under the guarantee provision, provincial securities would be as acceptable as other federally guaranteed securities in the portfolios of financial institutions. This would tend to broaden the market for provincial securities at home as well as reduce their cost in interest terms.

The other component in the policy of achieving a relative medium-term balance in the current account would be for the federal government to borrow abroad directly in order to finance temporary deficits on current account. This is what happened in 1978 but, unlike our proposal, that policy was not accompanied by other measures designed to bring the current account to surplus.

Conclusion

The importance of the international balance of payments has become obvious to Canadians. But since 1975 policymakers have failed to use the international sector to achieve domestic objectives. No goals were set for the balance of payments position, and the policy decisions in mid-1970s—first to encourage foreign borrowing, then to pursue a monetary policy that resulted in high interest rates because of its monetarist goal of slowing growth in the money supply—were inappropriate. Such policies resulted in a spiral of foreign debt and increased interest payments, causing further debt and a downward spiral in the external value of the Canadian dollar.

The objective for Canada in the 1980s must be to achieve a viable balance of payments position with a surplus on current account by mid-decade. Over the medium term, the goal of a balance on current account should be adopted, and structural policies should be implemented to shift the economy to produce both for export and to replace imported goods.

The capital account policy must conform to this current account strategy. Disruptive foreign borrowing, as in 1976, should not be allowed because of the longer-term economic hardships that follow. Programmes to ensure Canadian intermediation, when there are adequate savings in Canada, are necessary. The major energy projects planned for the early 1980s could be as disruptive to the Canadian economy as the massive provincial borrowings in 1976 if they were to be financed solely abroad. But such disruptions would be both unnecessary and unwarranted, for Canadians have adequate savings.

Conclusion
7

Something went wrong with Canada's economy in the last half of the 1970s. As a result, in mid-1979 the nation faces a fifth and possibly a sixth consecutive year of unsatisfactory economic performance. Economic growth lagged in three of the four years ending in 1978, and forecasts for 1979 and 1980 are for continued slow growth. The unemployment rate drifted higher through most of the late 1970s, and in early 1979 it stood at close to 8 per cent. Consumer prices increased 10.1 per cent in 1975, continued to rise sharply in later years, and rose 9 per cent in 1978. Finally, Canada's international balance of payments worsened over this period, despite a significantly depreciated Canadian dollar after 1976. Ironically, this half decade of poor economic performance coincided with the implementation of a significant series of innovative policies that attempted to alleviate these difficulties. The new monetary policy was labelled "monetarism."

The Adoption of Monetarist Policy
Canada's move to monetarism was a reaction to both international and domestic developments. After 1973 central banks in western industrialized countries were widely criticized for failing to contain the wave of international inflation triggered by the commodity and energy price boom of 1973 and 1974. In Canada influential economists argued that the expansionary monetary policies of the early 1970s exacerbated inflation, particularly because the Bank of Canada had paid too little attention to monetary aggregates. They argued that less inflation would have resulted from slower growth in the money supply. The political environment was shifting to the right because of concerns over inflation and the excessive growth of government. Such a climate was conducive to the adoption of a new anti-inflationary monetary policy.

In a speech in Saskatoon in 1975 Bank of Canada Governor Bouey announced an important change in the direction of Canada's monetary policy. Henceforth the determining factor in monetary policy in Canada would be the long-term commitment to lowering the inflation rate. Previously the Bank had been preoccupied with short-term stabilization objectives pursued primarily through its influence on interest rates and credit conditions. The new monetarist goals were different, for they focused on the longer term and used money supply growth targets as specific and appropriate goals for Bank policy.

Monetarism implies much more than a substitution of money supply growth objectives for the goal of achieving appropriate credit conditions. Under monetarism, which is associated with many economic assumptions, short-run goals are abandoned as the strict monetarist sees no practical use for fiscal or monetary stabilization measures. Monetarist policies are more concerned with inflation than unemployment, based on the assumption that unemployment has a natural level largely unaffected by policy measures. The Bank of Canada, however, embraced only the money supply targets and longer-term inflation objectives of monetarism and by implication, gave less weight to unemployment goals. In certain instances, however, such as their exchange rate intervention in 1978 and 1979, the Bank's actions contravened strict monetarist principles.

Monetarism and Economic Performance

The introduction of monetarist central banking principles occurred in a period when overall economic policy had never been as complex. Generously expansive fiscal measures, such as the inflation indexing of personal income tax brackets and exemptions, were introduced as was the indexing of social assistance payments. There were major cuts in personal and corporate income tax rates as well as a temporary reduction in provincial sales taxes and a major cut in the federal manufacturers' sales tax. Equally important were several policies that gave priority to reducing the growth of government spending as a means of reducing deficits and curbing the influence of governments on the national economy.

In addition to these changes in fiscal policy, a three-pronged attack on inflation was set in motion in late 1975. This programme included the setting-up of the Anti-Inflation Board to monitor and limit wage, price, and profit increases. A second measure was the deliberate scaling down of the growth of government spending as an anti-inflation measure. Finally, a "monetarist" monetary policy was introduced that emphasized the long-term goal of gradually lowering the rate of inflation by reducing the rate of growth in the money supply.

In late 1976, a year after the adoption of the monetarist strategy, the external value of the Canadian dollar began a prolonged and steep decline. Throughout 1977 and 1978 successive lows were reached, culminating in early 1979 with the Canadian dollar trading at a little above U.S. $0.83. During this period the Bank, acting on behalf of the federal government, directly intervened in the exchange market and, in 1978 alone, about $5 billion of newly borrowed exchange reserves were sold to rescue the falling dollar. In addition, throughout 1978 and 1979 a series of announcements of interest rate hikes was made by the Bank, prompted by interest rate increases in the United States and a desire to maintain an appropriate interest rate structure to support the external value of the Canadian dollar. By mid-1979 it appeared that the Canadian dollar had recovered from its low level and that interest rates, though still rising, were approaching a peak.

The economic performance of the Canadian economy in the second half of the 1970s was profoundly affected by the switch to anti-inflation goals and monetarism. The adoption of monetarism was parallelled by a consistent rise in unemployment until late 1978, without much compensating reduction in inflation. Because inflation did not moderate as expected, the Bank's adherence to a low rate of growth in the money supply acted to constrict the domestic economy between 1975 and 1978 and helps explain why the economy stagnated (Table 7-1). As a result, despite attempts to reduce government spending, the federal deficit soared, for the indexing of personal income tax exemptions and tax brackets made government revenues rise less rapidly while indexed social assistance benefits kept spending increasing by at least the rate of inflation.

A key part of the slowing of the economy was the detrimental effect of the new monetary strategy on Canada's balance of payments. Initially, the external value of the dollar rose dramatically, restricting both capital investment and the growth of domestic industries. Subsequently, the external value of the dollar fell to very low levels, but the international current account remained in a serious deficit position. The massive international borrowings in 1976, directly attributable to policy objectives and actions, had forced the current account into deficit, and the interest payments on that debt compounded the difficulties in bringing the current account back into balance.

75

TABLE 7-1
**RATE OF CHANGE IN THE REAL MONEY SUPPLY AND REAL
GNP, 1967-78**

| | Real Money Supply (M1) | | Real GNP | |
	Using GNE Deflator	Using Consumer Price Index	Annual	Four-Year Average
	(Per cent)			
1967	5.8	6.1	3.3	
1968	1.1	0.4	5.8	
1969	2.8	2.6	5.3	
1970	−2.5	−1.1	2.5	4.3
1971	9.5	9.8	6.9	
1972	9.3	9.5	6.1	
1973	5.4	6.9	7.5	
1974	−5.7	−1.2	3.6	6.0
1975	2.9	2.8	1.3	
1976	−1.6	0.6	5.5	
1977	1.4	0.3	2.7	
1978	3.4	1.1	3.4	3.2

Source: Department of Finance, *Economic Review* (April 1979), Tables 5, 45, 47, and 87.

The Failure of Monetarism

Why did monetarism fail? First, the adoption of monetarist goals, which encouraged the Bank of Canada to concentrate on long-term inflation effects, limited the effectiveness of the Bank's short-term stabilization role. Second, because of large capital inflows and the compounding effects of interest paid abroad, economic policies, including the new monetarism, failed to deliver a viable balance of payments position for Canada. The support of the external value of the Canadian dollar especially in 1978 focused on financing the large current account deficit rather than curing it. Third, because policymakers did not appreciate the structural nature of Canada's inflation, the Bank's adoption of money supply targets produced too low a rate of growth in the real money supply and this restrained the growth of the economy. Had the rate of inflation declined as expected in 1977 and 1978, better real economic growth would have materialized.

Most explanations of Canada's inflation in the 1970s recognized a series of extraordinary special factors such as accelerating food prices, the depreciation of the Canadian dollar, high money wage and salary settlements, and sharply rising energy prices, all of which were highly inflationary. But recognition of those factors did not lead to effective policy decisions.[1] To reduce inflation policymakers should have considered wage and salary increases and energy price escalations separately, since neither of these inflationary factors is greatly influenced by tight economic conditions. The independence of these two factors from monetary and fiscal policies means that such measures are not likely to efficiently correct structural inflation problems. Indeed, these structural factors would prevent the economy from returning to the lower rates of inflation and unemployment of the past, even if the economy were deliberately held in a prolonged slump.

Another failure of economic policy in this period relates to Canada's international payments position. In 1976 Ottawa encouraged capital inflows that pushed the external value of the Canadian dollar higher and forced the current account into a large deficit. At that time policymakers did not appear to realize that the rising current account deficit would perpetuate future deficits, exacerbate high unemployment, and increase the government fiscal deficit. Nor did they realize the difficult transition required to balance the current account. The neglect of an effective strategy for a current account balance not only retarded growth, but it also left the economy with high unemployment that may require years to reduce.

Problems for the Eighties

Canada's economic outlook for the 1980s remains clouded by a host of leftover macroeconomic problems of the late-1970s: high unemployment, high inflation, and an unsatisfactory trade-off between the two. Indeed, most medium-term projections conclude that high unemployment will continue into the early 1980s, despite an expected slowing in the labour force growth rate. A major part of any solution to the high unemployment low growth syndrome must be a reversal of the current account deficit in the balance of international payments. Canada must set a goal of a balanced current account in the medium term and accordingly expand Canadian industry to produce for both domestic and foreign markets. The large-scale capital requirements for the development of energy resources in the 1980s should not be allowed to deter pursuit of the goal of a balanced current account.

In their search for lower borrowing costs, provincial governments and agencies have in the past contributed substantially to Canada's balance of payments problem and, through the exchange rate, slowed domestic economic growth. In future, should such borrowings reach the

77

massive and disturbing size attained in 1976, some method of limiting the use of foreign capital markets by Canadians will have to be developed. Greater reliance on domestic capital by the provinces and their agencies would result in a broader and deeper capital market and would provide long-term benefits to Canada.

In preparing this study, we faced the problem of attempting to know what the Bank of Canada's intentions were when policies were introduced or changed. The Bank was more open and frank with the public in the last decade than in the past, but even more disclosure of policy intentions would improve Canadians' knowledge of their economy and financial system. Appendix B reviews the U.S. system of disclosure of monetary policy and suggests that it provides some useful ideas that could be modified for adoption in Canada.

Major Recommendations

Our review of the performance of monetary policy in the late 1970s leads to the following observations and recommendations.

- Monetary policy, after four years of monetarist strategy, failed to move the economy any closer to macroeconomic goals that had been attained prior to the 1975 change in policy direction. Indeed, in the last half of the 1970s economic performance was the worst in forty years. Monetary policy and the new monetarist doctrine must take at least some responsibility for this dismal performance. As the pre-eminent principle of monetary policy the monetarist doctrine should be discarded. At present the Bank of Canada's monetary policy objectives are stated in terms of money supply targets. Under the target-setting procedure, interest rates are administered in order to achieve the desired growth of the narrowly defined money supply. But even ignoring the foreign exchange effects, the level of short-term interest rates is more important than monetarists are willing to acknowledge.
  RECOMMENDATION: Bank of Canada goals should be set more flexibly in terms of interest rates, credit conditions, and money supply targets, with short-run priority given to interest rates and credit conditions.
- Canada in the 1970s faced a major policy dilemma in that the old trade-offs between inflation and unemployment no longer seemed to apply and thus policy options worsened. Both the energy price increases and the inability of wage and salary increases to moderate below a 7 to 8 per cent rate despite high unemployment have

78

been identified in this study as a major cause of structural inflation. This structural inflation is likely to persist into the 1980s. Monetary policy is an inefficient tool to combat the current wave of structural inflation. New policies must be formulated to deal with rigidities that inhibit wage, salary, and price de-escalation. Such policies would add to the efficiency of existing monetary and fiscal measures. A type of income policy seems to be called for, but Canada's experience with both voluntary and mandatory controls was unsatisfactory.

RECOMMENDATION: A tax-based incomes policy (TIP) should be examined carefully as a possible supplementary anti-inflation measure for Canada. Such a plan would use the federal corporate tax system to limit high wage or salary increases and would directly tackle one aspect of structural inflation. The plan, although not fully tested, should be administratively efficient and would likely avoid the negative effects on investment and productivity that are normally associated with direct control of incomes.

- In the pursuit of its anti-inflation objective, the goal of a viable balance of payments position appears to have been forgotten by Canadian policymakers after 1975. The result has been a rising current account deficit that may reach $7 to $8 billion in 1979 and 1980, unless new policies are introduced. That deficit implies massive foreign borrowings that will only serve to further exacerbate future current account deficits through additional future interest payments. A basic tenet of monetarism is that the balance of payments will look after itself and hence no direct policy actions are required. The absence of a goal and a viable strategy for Canada's international current account was seriously detrimental to economic performance in the late 1970s and is similarly unsuitable for the 1980s.

RECOMMENDATION: Canadian authorities should now aim to achieve a relative balance in the current account in the medium term. This means that deficits on current account in some years should be matched by surpluses in other years. When possible, surpluses should occur when the economy is weak; deficits, when the economy is strong. Achieving the goal of a medium-term balance on current account would result in no net losses or gains of jobs and output to the rest of the world.

- In some years, particularly 1976, borrowings in foreign markets by Canadian provinces, provincial agencies, municipalities, and corporations were so large that they adversely affected the level of the

exchange rate and forced the international current account into
deficit.

RECOMMENDATION: Canada's strategy should be to prevent
the international capital account from forcing the current account
into deficit. Provincial government and other financing abroad,
including the capital required for energy projects in the 1980s,
should not be allowed to affect adversely Canada's balance of
payments or the exchange rate. With proper timing, the reintrod-
uction of a withholding tax on all interest payments on long-term
securities issued abroad should be considered, as well as the rein-
statement of the guideline in force from 1970 to 1974 that Canadian borrowers search out domestic sources of funds before considering a long-term foreign issue. If external financing is deemed
appropriate for the economy, the federal government, rather than
the provinces or other borrowers, should be the principal issuer of
securities in foreign markets.

- A restriction on the placement of Canadian bond issues in foreign
markets should be regarded as an opportunity to improve Canadian capital markets. Most serious studies have shown that Canada
can produce the necessary savings to provide almost all the capital
for its future investment needs. Moreover we stress that, for Canada's policymakers, there were costs and inefficiencies because of
excessive international intermediation. Institutional changes should
be introduced to increase access to certain restricted pools of capital in Canada.

RECOMMENDATION: To widen and deepen the domestic market for Canadian provincial securities, provincial treasury bills
should be included in the list of eligible assets for the secondary
reserves required at the chartered banks. Moreover, Bank of Canada open market operations could be carried out just as efficiently
if they included the purchase and sale of provincial as well as
federal securities. Thus the Bank should include provincial securities in its asset holdings.

- There continues to be a scarcity of information on monetary policy
despite a substantial improvement over the past decade. This is
especially true regarding the formulation of monetary policy, the
view of the Bank on the economic prospects of the country, and
whether such a view is consistent with that of the Department of
Finance. It would improve the understanding and evaluation of
monetary policy if such information were available. The present

U.S. system on disclosure is vastly superior to Canada's in terms of candour and debate.

RECOMMENDATION: Additional information on the formulation of monetary policy should be made available to the public. A disclosure system such as that used by the U.S. Federal Reserve System would achieve this end. A similar framework, which would be consistent with Canada's political system and central banking structure, could be adapted for use in Canada.

APPENDIX A

Some Technical Problems in Setting Money Supply Targets

There are numerous technical problems related both to setting money supply targets and to predicting the impact of changes in the money supply on the economy. Among these problems are the choice of an appropriate definition of the money supply, the relationship of that definition to inflation and real economic growth, and the ability of the central bank to achieve the money supply goal in a manageable time frame.

Selecting the Appropriate Definition for the Money Supply

There is a variety of definitions of money supply, ranging from the very narrow to ones that include a broad range of financial assets. The Bank of Canada chose for its policy targets the narrowly defined money supply, which includes currency in the hands of the public and demand deposits at the chartered banks, usually abbreviated as M1. A slightly broader definition called M1B includes all of the items in M1 plus the chequable savings deposits at the chartered banks. A broader definition yet, M2, includes the items in M1B plus notice and term deposits at the chartered banks. And an even broader definition is M3, which includes currency in the hands of the public plus all the privately held chartered bank deposits.

There are serious policy limitations to almost any definition of money supply, since they all fail to measure the liquidity available to individuals and to predict the spending decisions of individuals and businesses. These definitions of the money supply differ only in terms of the amount of chartered bank liabilities included. All of them exclude the chequable deposits at the non-bank financial intermediaries such as the trust companies, the credit unions, and the caisses populaires. They also exclude the major unused source of purchasing power that exists in the credit available under bank credit card schemes.

82

The various money supplies have grown at markedly different rates, causing some embarrassment to the supporters of monetarism in Canada (Table A-1). Between 1976 and 1978, M1 recorded relatively low rates of growth of 10 per cent or less, but M3 continued to grow at annual rates of 14 to 18 per cent. Critics could therefore state that the Bank's policies were too expansionary using the M3 definition or too restrictionist based on the M1 definition.

Relationship to Real Economic Activity and Inflation

Monetarists maintain that there is a close relationship between growth in the money supply and growth in nominal GNP. But from Table A-1 it can be seen that it is difficult to associate changes in any one definition of the money supply to changes in the other economic indicators. In 1974, for example, M1 grew 9.6 per cent, M3 at 24.8 per cent, nominal GNP increased almost 20 per cent, and real GNP only 3.6 per cent. In 1978, however, M1 grew 10.1 per cent and nominal GNP advanced 10.3 per cent, but real economic growth was about the same as in 1974.

One of the ways of considering the effects of the money supply on the economy can be illustrated with the calculations of the National Income and Gross National Expenditure velocity of money figures set out in Table A-2. The change in the income velocity of money is considered a rough proxy for changes in the "demand for money," which refers to the hypothetical relationship between the desired amounts of money relative to the level of economic activity. It is usually assumed that increases in short-term interest rates provide an incentive to the public to economize on demand deposits and currency that yield no interest and to shift their money balances into interest-bearing time deposits. In a period of rising short-term interest rates one would expect to see some shifting of assets by the non-bank public as they substitute interest-bearing deposits for non-interest-bearing demand deposits. Thus interest rate changes affect the recorded income velocity of money and are used by the Bank of Canada to achieve its short-run objectives for M1.

The income velocity of money can also be affected by structural changes in the payments mechanism. In recent years there has been a more rapid growth in the chequing deposits at other financial institutions than at the chartered banks. Structural changes in the payments mechanism are often introduced with legislative changes such as the decennial revision of the Canadian Bank Act. These factors, and many others, affect the significance of a particular definition of the money

83

TABLE A-1
ANNUAL RATE OF CHANGE IN MONETARY AGGREGATES, NOMINAL AND REAL GNP, INFLATION, WAGES, AND ACTUAL UNEMPLOYMENT RATE, 1971-78

	Monetary Aggregates			GNP		Prices		Average Weekly Wages	Actual Unemployment Rate
	M1	M2	M3	Nominal	Real	GNE Deflator	Consumer Prices		
				(Per cent)					
1971	12.7	12.4	10.3	10.2	6.9	3.2	2.9	8.6	6.2
1972	14.3	10.6	14.0	11.4	6.1	5.0	4.8	8.4	6.2
1973	14.5	14.2	14.9	17.4	7.5	9.1	7.6	7.5	5.5
1974	9.6	20.1	24.8	19.4	3.6	15.3	10.8	11.0	5.3
1975	13.6	15.0	14.8	12.1	1.3	10.7	10.8	14.2	6.9
1976	8.1	12.5	18.3	15.8	5.5	9.7	7.5	12.2	7.1
1977	8.3	14.0	15.8	9.7	2.7	6.9	8.0	9.6	8.1
1978	10.1	10.7	13.7	10.3	3.4	6.7	9.0	6.2	8.4

Source: Department of Finance, *Economic Review* (April 1979), Tables 3, 5, 27, 42, 45, 47, and 87.

TABLE A-2
INCOME AND GNE VELOCITY OF MONEY, 1970-78

	NATIONAL INCOME divided by				GROSS NATIONAL EXPENDITURE divided by			
	M1	M1B	M2	M3	M1	M1B	M2	M3
	(Ratios)							
1970	7.05	4.34	2.50	1.99	9.40	5.79	3.34	2.65
1971	6.89	4.38	2.45	1.99	9.19	5.84	3.27	2.65
1972	6.79	4.37	2.50	1.96	8.96	5.78	3.30	2.59
1973	7.04	4.64	2.60	2.03	9.19	6.06	3.39	2.65
1974	7.73	5.27	2.60	1.96	10.02	6.84	3.37	2.54
1975	7.76	5.49	2.58	1.94	9.89	7.00	3.29	2.48
1976	8.25	5.94	2.64	1.89	10.59	7.62	3.38	2.42
1977	8.35	6.08	2.54	1.79	10.73	7.81	3.26	2.30
1978	8.40	6.19	2.54	1.74	10.75	7.91	3.25	2.23
75–1Q	7.85	5.50	2.57	1.93	10.03	7.03	3.29	2.46
2Q	7.73	5.45	2.55	1.94	9.90	6.97	3.26	2.48
3Q	7.85	5.55	2.61	1.97	9.94	7.03	3.30	2.49
4Q	7.62	5.46	2.60	1.94	9.70	6.95	3.31	2.48
76–1Q	8.05	5.76	2.66	1.94	10.32	7.39	3.42	2.49
2Q	8.36	6.01	2.69	1.92	10.68	7.68	3.44	2.45
3Q	8.24	5.95	2.62	1.86	10.59	7.65	3.36	2.39
4Q	8.36	6.04	2.58	1.84	10.76	7.77	3.32	2.36
77–1Q	8.34	6.04	2.53	1.80	10.78	7.81	3.27	2.33
2Q	8.39	6.11	2.54	1.80	10.74	7.83	3.26	2.30
3Q	8.37	6.10	2.54	1.79	10.71	7.81	3.25	2.28
4Q	8.32	6.07	2.53	1.77	10.68	7.79	3.25	2.27
78–1Q	8.36	6.08	2.52	1.76	10.78	7.84	3.26	2.27
2Q	8.51	6.23	2.57	1.77	10.86	7.96	3.28	2.26
3Q	8.46	6.26	2.57	1.76	10.77	7.97	3.27	2.23
4Q	8.28	6.17	2.49	1.68	10.59	7.89	3.18	2.15

Source: Calculated from Department of Finance, *Economic Review* (April 1979).

supply for general economic activity. Monetarists have no unequivocal answer to the question of which money supply should be used as a central bank target and leave policymakers with the practical question of choosing an appropriate definition.

Ability to Achieve Money Supply Targets

Once an appropriate money supply definition is selected, a central bank must be able to make changes quickly in the deposits that make up that statistic. The Bank of Canada has the ability to affect the level of cash reserves of the chartered banks and to force them to alter the growth rates in their total assets and liabilities. But the M1 definition of money supply constitutes a relatively small proportion of chartered banks' liabilities, and it is necessary for the Bank to effect a switch among the liabilities extended by the chartered banks in order to achieve its money supply targets. This is often achieved through changes in administered interest rates that encourage individuals and businesses to economize on cash balances when interest rates rise or to hold larger balances when interest rates fall. There are also many other factors that temporarily distort statistics on the size of the money supply, the most notable in recent years being two postal strikes that resulted in a ballooning of M1.

In the very short term, changes in the seasonal payments pattern or problems with sampling procedures can also distort the interpretation of the money supply statistics. The defined monthly money supply is an average of the Wednesday figures in that particular month. Occasionally Wednesday will coincide with peak days for demand deposits, such as the mid-month and end of month pay periods and distort the actual monthly figures.

It must also be remembered that the Bank is operating in the money markets on a day-to-day basis. But the most recent statistics available to them are a week to two weeks old and must be seasonally adjusted. Despite the precision that appears to be associated with money supply targets, there are substantial grey areas requiring judgment in interpreting the statistics and in attempting to reach targets.

APPENDIX B

The Disclosure Issue

For some time we have been concerned that the flow of information and the dialogue between the critics and supporters of monetary policy have been hampered by institutional practices that restrict information. Information that is unavailable includes reports of the internal deliberations of the Bank of Canada on policy matters; the Bank's analysis and outlook for the economy; the interrelations between the Department of Finance and the Bank; and dissenting opinions on policy within government. Because of our concern, we have examined the information available in the United States about monetary policy and its formation as a possible example of more open policies that could be adopted in Canada.

U.S. Practice

Disclosure to the public of the monthly deliberations of the Federal Reserve System's Open Market Committee (the FOMC) and its policy directive to the Federal Reserve Bank of New York are an integral part of U.S. monetary policy. And there is a trend in the United States now towards even more frequent and substantive disclosure of monetary issues. At this time there is a degree of openness with the public over the Federal Reserve System's expectations for the economy, particularly about economic growth, the balance of payments, unemployment, and inflation. In addition, the objectives and targets for the various monetary policy instruments—specifically, the federal funds rate and money supply growth target rates—are recorded for the public.

In the United States, the FOMC is the centre of policy decisions and the vehicle for disclosure. The FOMC is directly involved in monetary policy through the open market operations of the Federal Reserve System—that is, the buying and selling of U.S. government and federal agency securities and bankers' acceptances. Open market policy does not represent the entire range of the tools available to the Federal Reserve System in the monetary area, but open market operations are acknowledged to be a prime monetary lever. Other major monetary policy tools are changes in commercial bank reserve requirements set by the Board of Governors of the Federal Reserve System and changes in discount rates established by the boards of directors of the twelve regional Federal Reserve banks.

The FOMC consists of twelve members, seven of whom are drawn from the Federal Reserve Board and five of whom are Federal Reserve bank presidents. By tradition, the chairman of the Board of Governors is also the chairman of the FOMC. The president of the New York Federal Reserve Bank is a permanent member of the Committee, since that Bank carries out the actual instructions of the FOMC.

The Committee meets regularly once each month to discuss economic trends and to decide upon the future course of open market operations. At these meetings some of the most important elements in the Federal Reserve System's monetary policy are formulated. Obviously, there are additional interchanges among FOMC members, but it is at these formal meetings policymaking is recorded:

> During each regular meeting, a directive was issued to the Federal Reserve Bank of New York stating the general economic goals of the Committee and providing general guidelines as to how the manager of the System Open Market Account at the New York Federal Reserve Bank should conduct Open Market operations to achieve these goals.... The decisions on the exact timing and amount of daily buying and selling of securities in fulfilling the Committee's directive are the responsibility of the System Open Market Account manager at the trading desk of the New York Bank.[1]

Disclosure procedures did not arise completely spontaneously in the U.S. Federal Reserve System, but rather were prompted by congressional criticisms and concerns about Federal Reserve policy targets and mechanisms. Indeed, many of these criticisms were voiced because it was thought too little "formal" attention was being placed on the monetary aggregates.

Another type of disclosure involves testimony before U.S. congressional committees. The policy of announcing longer run tolerance ranges for the major monetary aggregates began in early 1975 after Congress passed a formal resolution requesting that the Board of Governors consult with committees of the Congress on a quarterly basis with respect to its monetary objectives and plans for the range of growth of monetary aggregates over the next twelve months.[2] Since that date the chairman of the Federal Reserve System has been meeting regularly with congressional committees at about ninety-day intervals.

In his quarterly presentations to the House and Senate Banking Committees, the chairman of the Federal Reserve Bank announces projected growth ranges for monetary aggregates for the coming four calendar quarters. The targets are set in terms of numerical ranges for two definitions of the money supply, as well as a bank credit measure. The monetary targets set in this way are M1 (currency plus demand deposits) and M2 (M1 plus commercial bank time and savings deposits other than large negotiable certificates of deposit).

The FOMC objectives, which are relayed to the trading desk of the New York Federal Reserve Bank, are stated with a series of similar tolerance ranges for money supply and interest rates. Money supply targets are stated on a seasonally adjusted annual growth rate basis from the month before the meeting to the month after the meeting. The FOMC also indicates how the manager is to vary his objective for the federal funds rate if incoming data cause revisions in the projections of M1 and M2 relative to the ranges. In 1976 the FOMC decided to release its short-term operating targets for monetary aggregates and the federal funds rate with a shorter delay than had previously been the case. Between mid-1967 and early 1975 there had been a delay of about ninety days in releasing a "Record" of each FOMC meeting. Early in 1975 this interval was shortened to forty-five days, and at the May 1, 1976, meeting, the FOMC voted to release its Record with a delay of only one month.

From our perspective, the summaries of the Committee's "Record of Policy Actions" are of special interest. These records are released thirty days after the meeting and are published both in the annual report of the Board of Governors of the Federal Reserve System every spring and in the *Federal Reserve Bulletin* each month. As the Federal Reserve Bank of St. Louis noted in a review of the 1977 FOMC decisions, the summaries generally include:

1) a staff summary of recent economic developments, such as prices, employment, industrial production, and components of the national income accounts; and projections concerning real output growth for two or three quarters ahead;
2) a discussion of recent international financial developments and the United States foreign trade balance;

3) a discussion of recent credit market conditions and recent interest rate movements;
4) a discussion of open market operations, the growth of monetary aggregates, and bank reserve and money market conditions since the previous meeting;
5) a discussion of current policy considerations, including money market conditions and the movements of monetary aggregates;
6) conclusions of the FOMC;
7) a policy directive issued by the Committee to the Federal Reserve Bank of New York;
8) a list of the members' voting positions and any dissenting comments;
9) a description of any actions and consultations that may have occurred between the regularly scheduled meetings.[3]

It is important to realize that there is a deliberate attempt to integrate the longer-term policy goals, the twelve-month projections, with the short-term targets. The instructions provided to the Open Market Account manager at the trading desk are stated in terms of money market conditions and near-term rates of growth of M1 and M2 considered to be consistent with the desired longer-run growth rates of monetary aggregates.

Table B-1 reproduces a summary of 1977 operating ranges and targets as assembled by the Federal Reserve Bank of St. Louis. As well, the summary reports include a brief statement by dissenting members of the Open Market Committee. The dissensions provide valuable information about the goals and frustrations of members of the U.S. central bank. At the September 20 session, two Committee members—Tilby and Wallich—dissented from the majority opinion, as the Committee directive to the Federal Reserve Bank of New York trading desk allowed for more interest rate firming than they thought appropriate at that time.

A more detailed excerpt from the Record of Policy Actions of the Federal Open Market Committee at the May 16, 1978, meeting is included here. At that meeting a summary of the Domestic Policy Directive discussion was set out. The discussion touched on many topics, including staff economic projections for the year ahead, recent economic trends, actions taken by the manager of the System Open Market Account during the previous month, staff projections of financial conditions for M1 and M2, and differences in opinion on consumer spending and inflation. The following quotation represents part of the directive issued to the Federal Reserve Bank of New York based on that meeting:

... the Committee decided that the ranges of tolerance for the annual rates of growth in M1 and M2 over the May-June period should be 3 to 8 and 4 to 9 per cent, respectively. It was understood that in assessing the behavior of these aggregates the Manager should continue to give approximately equal weight to the behavior of M1 and M2.... The members agreed that if growth rates of the aggregates over the 2-month period appeared to be deviating significantly from the midpoints of the indicated ranges, the operational objective for the weekly-average Federal funds rate should be modified in an orderly fashion within a range of 7 1/4 to 7 3/4 per cent.[4]

At the meeting, Mr. Willis dissented from the operating instructions, as "he favoured more vigorous measures to reduce the rate of monetary growth, given the acceleration of the rate of inflation and its adverse effect on consumer and business confidence and spending plans. Specifically, he preferred a range of 2 1/2 to 6 1/2 per cent for the annual rate of growth in M1 over the May-June period and an inter-meeting range of 7 1/4 to 8 per cent for the Federal funds rate."[5]

A Disclosure Policy for Canada

It is difficult to discuss disclosure policy in Canada, since practices here are deliberately vague. While the Bank of Canada pursues a similar monetary aggregate strategy to the U.S. Federal Reserve System, neither the frequency of review nor the analysis of economic conditions is made public in Canada.

Paul A. Volcker, formerly president of the Federal Reserve Bank of New York and in 1979 chairman of the Federal Reserve Board, noted in a speech to the Toronto Bond Traders' Association on February 22, 1977, that "unlike the Federal Reserve, the Bank of Canada targets only one of the monetary aggregates—the narrowly defined money stock, M1. Targets have generally not been reviewed publicly as frequently as in the United States."[6]

The Bank of Canada makes presentations to parliamentary committees, but detailed information especially about intent and dissension—such as is available in the monthly FOMC Record—never reaches the public. Policy pronouncements originate in press releases, speeches, the annual report of the Governor of the Bank of Canada to the Minister of Finance, or other statements.

As a general principal, more disclosure to the interested public of the actual deliberations on monetary policy would be in the national interest. Greater disclosure in a form similar to that in the United States would result in several changes.

TABLE B-1
UNITED STATES FOMC OPERATING GROWTH RANGES AND TARGETS, 1977

Short-Run Ranges[1]

Date of Meeting	Federal Funds Rate Range	Initial Federal Funds Rate Target	Period to which M1 & M2 apply	Ranges Specified M1	Ranges Specified M2	Actual Growth Rates M1	Actual Growth Rates M2
January 17-18[a]	4¼-5%	4⅝-4¾%	Jan.-Feb.	3-7%	7-11%	3.1%	8.4%
February 15	4¼-5	4⅝-4¾	Feb.-Mar.	3-7	6½-10½	3.1	7.9
March 15	4¼-5¼	4⅝-4¾	Mar.-Apr.	4½-8½	7-11	12.4	11.1
April 19	4½-5¼	4¾	Apr.-May	6-10	8-12	10.1	9.1
May 6[2]	4½-5½	5¼					
May 17	5¼-5¾	5⅜	May-June	0-4	3½-7½	2.6	6.4
June 21[b]	5¼-5¾	5⅜	June-July	2½-6½	6-10	11.4	12.4
July 19	5¼-5¾	5⅜	July-Aug.	3½-7½	6½-10½	12.1	11.6
August 5[2]	5¼-6	5¾					
August 16	5¾-6¼	6	Aug.-Sept.	0-5	3- 8	6.6	7.2
September 20[c]	6-6½	6¼	Sept.-Oct.	2-7	4- 8	9.7	9.1
October 17-18[d]	6¼-6¾	6½	Oct.-Nov.	3-8	5½- 9½	5.3	7.4
November 15	6¼-6¾	6½	Nov.-Dec.	1-7	5- 9	3.1	5.2
December 19-20[e]	6¼-6¾	6½	Dec.-Jan.	2½-8½	6-10	7.4	7.0
January 9, 1978[2]	6½-7	6¾					

Longer-Run Ranges[3]

Date of Meeting	Target Period	M1	M2	M3	Credit Proxy[4]
January 17-18	IV/76-IV/77	4½-6½%	7-10%	8½-11½%	7-10%
April 19[f]	I/77-I/78	4½-6½	7- 9½	8½-11	7-10
July 19[g]	II/77-II/78	4-6½	7- 9½	8½-11	7-10[4]
October 17-18[h]	III/77-III/78	4-6½	6½- 9	8-10½	7-10

[1] Short-run ranges were adopted at each of the FOMC's regularly scheduled meetings. The ranges for the monetary aggregates were specified in terms of two-month simple annual rates of change from the month prior to the meetings at which the ranges were established to the month following the meeting. The ranges for the Federal funds rate were specified to cover the period from the meeting at which the ranges were adopted to the following regularly scheduled meeting. Short-run ranges were made available in the "Record of Policy Actions of the Federal Open Market Committee" approximately 30 days after each meeting.

[2] Telephone or telegram consultations were held between scheduled meetings for the purpose of modifying intermeeting ranges for the Federal funds rate.

[3] Chairman of the Federal Reserve Board Arthur F. Burns announced intended growth rates of monetary aggregates over the indicated one year periods in statements presented before Congressional Committees at intervals of approximately 90 days.

[4] At the July 19 meeting the Committee decided to replace bank credit proxy with a broader measure of all commercial bank credit. This change was due in part because of the growth in importance of nonmember banks (credit proxy is based on data solely for member banks) and in part because the proxy does not include certain borrowings by banks from the nonbank public.

[a] Mr. Balles dissented at this meeting because he believed that real GNP and prices now bore a closer relationship to the behavior of M2 than to that of M1. He was concerned that growth in M2 had been exceeding the Committee's longer-run range and about the consequent implications for future inflation. Therefore, he preferred a higher upper limit on the Federal funds rate range than was adopted, and preferred that the System aim initially for a funds rate of 4¾ instead of 4⅝-4¾.

[b] Mr. Coldwell dissented at this meeting because he favored a wider funds rate range of 5 to 5¾ percent, in order to provide more leeway for a reduction of the Federal funds rate should the rates of growth in M1 and M2 appear to be near or below the lower limits of their specified ranges for the June-July period.

[c] Messrs. Lilly and Wallich dissented at this meeting because the directive allowed more firming in money market conditions than they thought appropriate in view of their judgment that the economic situation was not very strong. In addition, Mr. Lilly believed that further tightening in money market conditions would not be effective in dealing with the underlying structural inflation. Messrs. Morris and Roos dissented on the grounds that the policy adopted represented an inadequate response to the rapid rates of monetary growth over recent months. Mr. Roos felt that, unless action was taken to reduce M1 growth now, inflation would accelerate and more drastic action would need to be taken later.

[d] Mr. Morris dissented at this meeting because he was convinced that the Committee should take more aggressive action to curb excessive growth in the monetary aggregates. He thought that short-term interest rates could rise further without significantly damaging short-term prospects for economic activity.

[e] Mr. Roos dissented at this meeting because he believed that the upper limit of the December-January range for growth in M1 allowed for the possibility of too rapid growth in that aggregate. In his opinion, M1 growth over this period at a rate in excess of 6½ percent would require an excessively restrictive policy later if the FOMC's longer-range growth targets were to be achieved.

[f] Mr. Partee dissented.

[g] Messrs. Coldwell, Jackson, and Roos dissented.

[h] Mr. Wallich dissented.

Source: Federal Reserve Bank of St. Louis, *Review* (March 1978), p. 3.

The Bank of Canada would be forced to operate internally and externally with a consistent outlook for the economy. If there were two different viewpoints on the economy, the public would have some insight into makeup, arguments, and implications of the various economic predictions. In a nutshell, the public prognostications on the economy would have to be consistent with the internal ones held by the Bank—and by the Department of Finance.

- It is generally accepted that governments and central banks should seek to reduce uncertainties. To the degree that interested observers would be operating—in theory—with an improved information base, decisions would have an extra degree of rationality to them. Thus, better informed business and government decisions should be possible within a framework of added disclosure.
- The Bank of Canada, like many central banks, can disguise its policies and goals behind a screen of limited public disclosure. As a result, evaluation of the Bank's objectives, targets, successes, and failures is difficult. With disclosure it would be less difficult to hold the Bank accountable for most of its actions.
- In a related way, if errors in policymaking were acknowledged, it would become possible for the public to pinpoint the source of the problem. For example, if the central bank chose to pursue a short-term interest rate target and it was not achieved, some evaluation would presumably be provided in the meetings and would be available to the public as well.
- In addition, better disclosure systems allow the outsider to attempt to disentangle causes of forecasting errors—that is, errors resulting from a misunderstanding of the way the economic system is operating—from errors that result from unforseen external events.

We are favourably impressed with the relatively more open disclosure about monetary policy in the United States. While it is difficult to pinpoint the precise manner in which the Bank of Canada formulates its policies, it is clear that the equivalent of a U.S. FOMC does not exist in Canada. Indeed, our traditions and practices are different.

In Canada, the Minister of Finance can, in theory, play a very important role in developing and implementing monetary policy. In practice this does not seem to have been the case, even though the 1967 Bank Act increased his power and responsibilities in the monetary policy area.

The Deputy Minister of Finance is a non-voting member of the

Board of Directors of the Bank of Canada, and the Minister of Finance has the authority to issue a directive to the Governor to adopt specific monetary policies. The Department of Finance can override the Bank and has an obligation to do so in cases of disagreement. As well, a Governor of the Bank could try and alter a directive through direct appearances before committees of Parliament or appeal his case to the general public. Since the 1967 Bank Act, which clarified the respective roles, no such directives have been issued. That is, compromise or agreement between the Department of Finance and the Bank of Canada have prevailed.

If disclosure were the practice in Canada, neither Cabinet secrecy nor autonomy need be compromised, since the role of the Department of Finance in monetary matters—with the possible exception of its role in foreign exchange management—is more negative than positive. That is, when Finance agrees with Bank of Canada policy, presumably it takes no action. Thus, greater and more frequent disclosure need not be viewed as a threat to the Department of Finance or the federal government, since Finance's role in monetary policymaking is indirect, rather than direct.

As a model for a Canadian system, we suggest that the U.S. FOMC meetings, which are reported to the public with a thirty-day delay, represent a system that seems to work well. The meeting is composed of a group of relative equals in terms of central bank policy; as much as possible, an equivalent Canadian committee should also be composed of similar senior central bank officials and others.

We do not think that the Board of Directors of the Bank of Canada represents the proper forum for such deliberations and disclosure. As presently constituted, the Board of Directors has two professional central bankers—the Governor and the Deputy Governor—while the remaining members are drawn from many fields and disciplines and cannot match the expertise of these two professionals. But, the Board could provide that proper forum if it were reconstituted to include a wider spectrum of economic opinion and additional senior Bank officials.

Our purpose in suggesting the U.S. model is that it provides a better framework for disclosure. The present U.S. system is vastly superior to Canada's because of the openness of debate, and a similar framework could be adapted for use consistent with Canada's central banking structure.

As to the specifics of disclosures, the topics included in the U.S. FOMC "Record" could be used as a target for a Canadian monthly information release. In that manner, the designated Canadian committee would disclose, with a one-month delay, their short-term economic objectives, shortfalls from targets, and short-term economic uncertainties. There would be discussion of alternative or dissenting viewpoints and the rationale behind the monetary policy and targets that were adopted.

Notes

Chapter 1

[1] Bank of Canada Act, R.S.C. 1952, c.13 as amended by R.S.C. 1952, c. 315; 1953-54, c. 33; and R.S.C. 1966-67, c. 88.

[2] *Ibid.*

[3] Bank of Canada, *Annual Report of the Governor to the Minister of Finance, 1971*, p. 7. The issue of capital inflows and current account deficits is explored in detail in chapter 6.

[4] Bank of Canada, *Annual Report of the Governor to the Minister of Finance, 1972*, p. 7.

[5] *Ibid.*

[6] *Ibid.* p. 10.

[7] Bank of Canada, *Annual Report of the Governor to the Minister of Finance, 1973*, p. 5.

[8] *Ibid.* p. 16.

[9] *Ibid.* p. 24.

[10] Canada imports crude oil from abroad, destined primarily for Quebec and the Maritime provinces. Western Canadian oil and gas are exported to the United States as is electricity. The net surplus in energy trade was $1.4 billion in 1977; $1.3 billion in 1976; $1.3 billion in 1975; $1.8 billion in 1974; $1.2 billion in 1973; and $0.7 billion in 1972. See Canadian Petroleum Association, *Statistical Handbook*, Section XI.

[11] See, for example, the Presidential Address to the Canadian Economics Association. Roger Dehem "Presidential Address: Living Beyond the Short Run," *Canadian Journal of Economics*, Vol. VII, No. 4 (November 1974).

[12] Two schools of thought should be noted particularly in terms of these criticisms. One stresses that the Bank must accommodate the government by monetizing its debt; hence, the central bank was reluctantly forced to increase the money supply. The other stresses the independence of the Bank to establish its own monetary goals; thus any monetizing of federal government debt was discretionary on the part of the Bank.

[13] Except, perhaps, during the "Coyne Affair" in the early 1960s. See David C. Smith and David W. Slater, "The Economic Policy Proposals of the Governor of the Bank of Canada," *Queen's Quarterly*, Vol. LXVIII, No. 1 (Spring 1960).

Chapter 2

[1] The literature on economic stabilization measures and the respective roles for monetary and fiscal policies is vast. An excellent and brief bibliography on some of the major issues in the debate in the United States was provided by F. Modigliani in his presidential address to the American Economic Association in Atlantic City, New

Jersey, in September 1976. See Franco Modigliani, "The Monetarist Controversy or Should We Forsake Stabilization Policies?" *American Economic Review*, Vol. 67, No. 2 (March 1977), pp. 18-19. Also comprehensive is A. Robert Nobay and Harry S. Johnson, "Monetarism: A Historic-Theoretic Perspective," *Journal of Economic Literature*, Vol. 15, No. 2 (June 1977), pp. 483-85.

2 See Thomas Courchene, *Money, Inflation, and the Bank of Canada: An Analysis of Canadian Monetary Policy from 1970 to Early 1975* (Montreal: C. D. Howe Research Institute, 1976); his *Monetarism and Controls: The Inflation Fighters* (Montreal: C. D. Howe Research Institute, 1976); and his *The Strategy of Gradualism: An Analysis of Bank of Canada Policy from Mid-1975 to Mid-1977* (Montreal: C. D. Howe Research Institute, 1978). See also remarks by G. E. Freeman, Deputy Governor of the Bank of Canada, *Bank of Canada Review* (December 1976). In fairness to the Bank authorities, their policy statements at no point explicitly use the expression monetarism, though their policies appear in principle to be identical.

3 Courchene, *Monetarism and Controls*, p. 111.

4 Courchene, *The Strategy of Gradualism*, p. 59. For a recent discussion of the role of money and exchange rate policies in Canada see Christoper A. Sarlo, "The Role of Money in the Canadian Economy: Fixed vs Flexible Exchange Rates," and William M. Scarth, "Real Disturbances, Perfect Capital Mobility and Exchange Rate Policy," *Canadian Journal of Economics*, Vol. XII, No. 1 (February 1979), pp. 89-100.

5 It is a pity that this type of critical analysis, as articulate and evocative as it is, supported the series of errors in the monetary management of the economy since 1975. For some reason the monetarist school refuses to deal with the unemployment issue, always treating unemployment—itself a function of slow real economic growth—as a temporary phenomenon resulting either from frictions or bottlenecks in labour markets, unemployment insurance legislation, or unadvisedly high minimum wages. There is no room in this framework for genuinely involuntary unemployment; nor for that matter, is there much recognition that tight money—as it affects the economy—has its earliest impact on the economy and often a delayed impact, if any, on inflation.

While Courchene and other monetarist proponents in Canada applaud the "gradualistic approach" of monetary policy, we suggest that the strategy of gradualism and monetary policy generally must be judged in terms of its real impact on the economy. Judged from that perspective, monetary tightening since 1975 was not gradualistic but heavy handed.

6 David Cobham has noted that a monetarist theory of inflation can in principle be supported by both left- and right-wing economists: "The economic mechanisms of inflation are politically neutral: it is not your monetarism or your anti-monetarism, but what you do with it, that is determined by your politics." See David Cobham, "The Politics of the Economics of Inflation," *Lloyds Bank Review*, No. 128 (April 1978), p. 32. Alternatively, Modigliani stresses the stabilization policy controversy, which at its core concerns the issue of government intervention. See Modigliani, "The Monetarist Controversy."

7 Modigliani, "The Monetarist Controversy," p. 1.

8 Nobay and Johnson, "Monetarism," p. 479.

9 Milton Friedman, "The Role of Monetary Policy," *American Economic Review*, Vol. 58, No. 1 (March 1968), pp. 1-17; and Edmund S. Phelps, *et al.*, *Microeconomic Foundation of Employment and Inflation Theory* (New York: Norton, 1970).

10 William J. Frazer, *Crisis in Economic Theory: A Study of Monetary Policy, Analysis and Economic Goals* (Gainesville: University of Florida Press, 1973), p. 350.

11 See Nobay and Johnson, "Monetarism," p. 479.

12 Modigliani, "The Monetarist Controversy," p. 18.

[13] The rational expectations literature is extensive. Two examples are Frederick S. Mishkin, "Efficient Markets Theory: Implications for Monetary Policy," *Brookings Papers on Economic Activity*, No. 3 (1978), pp. 708-67 and William Poole, "Rational Expectations in the Macro Model," *Brookings Papers on Economic Activity*, No. 2 (1976), pp. 463-513.

[14] Irving Fisher, *The Purchasing Power of Money* (New York: Macmillan, 1911). There is much evidence to support the Fisher principle as an explanation of movements in long-term interest rates. Many financial studies in both Canada and the United States suggest a fairly close correspondence between changes in inflationary expectations and changes in long-term interest rates.

[15] See Benjamin M. Friedman, "Crowding Out or Crowding In? Economic Consequences of Financing Government Deficits," *Brookings Papers on Economic Activity*, No. 3 (1978), pp. 593-654.

Chapter 3

[1] G. K. Bouey, Remarks to the Canadian Chamber of Commerce, 46th Annual Meeting Saskatoon, September 22, 1975. *Bank of Canada Review* (October 1975), pp. 28, 29.

[2] A series of commentaries published in the *Bank of Canada Review* in 1976 and 1977 cited the policy changes that the Bank of Canada intended to implement. See "Remarks by Gerald K. Bouey, Governor of the Bank of Canada," Saskatoon, October 1975; "Remarks by G. E. Freeman, Deputy Governor of the Bank of Canada," December 1976; "Remarks by Gerald K. Bouey, Governor of the Bank of Canada," September 1977.

[3] As is elaborated upon in chapter 6, Canada's international current account deficit can also be viewed as a result of international borrowing rather than a cause because the level of international borrowing can be considered largely autonomous and not the result of current account transactions. If the level of international borrowing is autonomous and not particularly related to the level of the exchange rate, then it follows that the level of Canada's exchange rate will affect the amount of goods and services bought and sold internationally. Thus if the exchange rate is too high because of large amounts of foreign capital being borrowed, the effect will be to encourage imports and discourage Canadian exports, throwing Canada's international current account into deficit. That deficit would be required to match the capital surplus caused by massive international borrowings. It must also be remembered that, in the short run, short-term capital movements can be made to offset the effects of long-term capital borrowings, and indeed long-term capital borrowings could be offset by increases in exchange holdings of the government. See also Richard G. Lipsey, "The Canadian Dollar: Problems and Prospects," The Ryerson Lectures in Economics, Toronto, January 16, 1978; C. R. McConnell and W. H. Pope, *Economics* (Toronto: McGraw Hill Ryerson, 1978), ch. 42; and D. E. Bond and R. A. Shearer, *The Economics of the Canadian Financial System: Theory, Policy and Institutions* (Scarborough: Prentice-Hall Canada, 1972), p. 551.

[4] If a discomfort index were broadened to include additional statistics of generally accepted policy targets—such as employment growth, economic growth, and relative size of the current account deficit in the balance of payments—a similar negative conclusion would hold for the post-1975 years.

[5] In theory, perfectly flexible exchange rates permit central banks to pursue their own independent monetary posture. In the current instance Canada has synchronized its interest rate policies with those of the United States, largely abandoning this separate option.

Chapter 4

[1] As discussed in chapter 2, the Phillips curve traces a series of combinations of rates of unemployment and of price increases. The curve illustrates that higher rates of unemployment are associated with lower rates of inflation and vice versa.

[2] In mid-1979 the unemployment rate may not be an appropriate measure of cyclicality for the Canadian economy, as many firms in the industrial sector are operating near capacity despite an 8 per cent national unemployment rate.

[3] It is possible to ignore the effects of external inflation on the assumption that in the long run the exchange rate will adjust to the relative difference between national and international inflation rates. To the degree that international inflation is independent of the domestic economy, then the exchange rate is truly set by domestic inflation and the policies that affect it.

[4] This argument is, in our view, consistent with the theoretical belief that, in the long run, inflation is a purely monetary phenomenon. In the short run, money supply changes may not predominate in the determination of the pace of inflation.

[5] Department of Finance, *Canada's Recent Inflation Experience* (Ottawa, 1978), p. 6.

[6] The consumer price index from 1962 to 1978 rose at an average annual rate of 5.4 per cent. The index excluding food rose at a 5.0 per cent annual rate and the food index rose at a 6.4 per cent rate over that sixteen-year period.

[7] Sidney Weintraub, "The Missing Theory of Money Wages," *Journal of Post Keynesian Economics*, Vol. 1, No. 2 (Winter 1978-79), pp. 59-78.

[8] This has been close to the case in Germany, Switzerland, and Japan during the past few years because the value of their currencies has risen sharply in foreign markets.

[9] It is not our purpose to evaluate energy policy, particularly the distortions and subsidies inherent in a stable price option. It may be that such distortions are more desirable than the implied inflation of the other options. It does appear, however, that Canadian policymakers in mid-1979 have not chosen the option of stable energy prices.

[10] There already exists a very extensive literature on tax-based incomes policies. The original 1971 article that sparked the interest of professional economists and public officials was written by Henry Wallich and Sidney Weintraub. See H. Wallich, and S. Weintraub, "A Tax-Based Incomes Policy," *Journal of Economic Issues*, 5 (June 1971), pp. 1-19. See also L. Dildine, and E. Sunley, "Administrative Problems of Tax-Based Incomes Policies" *Brookings Papers on Economic Activity*, 2, (1978), pp. 363-89; A. Okun, and G. Perry, (eds). "Innovative Policies to Slow Inflation." *Brookings Papers on Economic Activity*, 2 (1978); J. Pechman, "Comment on the Dildine-Sunley Paper," *Brookings Papers on Economic Activity*, 2 (1978), pp. 390-94; G. Perry, "Slowing the Wage-Price Spiral: The Macroeconomic View," *Brookings Papers on Economic Activity*, 2 (1978), pp. 259-91; L. Seidman, "A New Approach to the Control of Inflation," *Challenge*, 19 (July/August 1976), pp. 39–43. L. Seidman, "Tax-Based Incomes Policies," *Brookings Papers on Economic Activity*, 2 (1978), pp. 301-48; L. Seidman, "Would Tax Shifting Undermine the Tax-Based Incomes Policy?" *Journal of Economic Issues*, 12 (September 1978), pp. 647-76; L. Seidman, "TIP: Feasibility and Equity," *Journal of Post Keynesian Economics*, 1 (Summer 1979), pp. 24-37; S. Weintraub "The Missing Theory of Money Wages," *Journal of Post Keynesian Economics*, 1 (Winter 1978-79), pp. 59-78.

[11] The TIP proposal is expanded upon in Sidney Weintraub, *Capitalism's Inflation and Unemployment Crisis: Beyond Monetarism and Keynesianism* (Reading, Mass.: Addison-Wesley, 1978).

[12] Abba P. Lerner, "Stagflation: Its Cause and Cure," *Challenge* (September/October, 1977), p. 15.

100

[13] Laurence S. Seidman suggests adding two additional features to the original Wallich-Weintraub TIP plan: "Real wage insurance—an automatically triggered, general tax rebate to all low and middle income households whenever the growth rate of the average real wage in the economy falls below the growth rate of average labour productivity in a given year; and profit restraint insurance—a uniform surtax, limited to the largest corporations (covered by TIP), imposed if the ratio of aggregate profit to aggregate labour compensation for the whole covered sector increases abnormally in a given year." While we acknowledge that these additional features would tend to moderate uncertainty that one group may be able to take advantage of another group as a result of TIP, in fact the problem facing the Canadian economy in the 1980s is that this period is expected to be very abnormal, primarily because of high relative inflation and low increases in labour productivity and real wages. We prefer, instead, our version of the original Weintraub-Wallich plan that would include a commitment by the federal government to ensure that additional fiscal measures would be introduced should the real purchasing power of labour appear to suffer disproportionately as a result of the TIP plan. See Seidman, "TIP: Flexibility and Equity," p. 37.

[14] In July 1979 the Canadian Institute for Economic Policy stated that some form of incomes policy was necessary in the present environment. The Institute tentatively advocated a selective incomes control programme aimed at key sectors of the economy that possess market power. One option they considered had several features in common with the modified TIP plan discussed in this study. "A possible alternative approach would be to require companies and trade unions in selected industries that wield monopoly power to justify their proposals for increases in prices and wages. They could be permitted to implement their proposals without the prior approval of the monitoring authority. But in that case, the authority should be required to recommend to the government a deterrent, such as the imposition of a surtax, to any irresponsible use of private monopoly power that would be contrary to the public interest." Canadian Institute for Economic Policy, *A Statement on Current Economic Issues* (July 1979), p. 11.

Chapter 5

[1] Economic Council of Canada, *Annual Review: A Time for Reason* (Ottawa: Supply and Services Canada, 1978), pp. 139-40.

[2] A rough measure of the job losses and the unemployment effect associated with the 1978 current account deficit can be calculated in the following way. In 1973, when the Canadian economy was approximately fully employed, every employed worker contributed $12,249 to real GNP. The 1978 current account deficit, expressed in national accounts terms and in real 1971 dollars, was $3,622 million, which translates into 298,000 jobs or 2.7 per cent of the 1978 labour force. Some additional growth in worker productivity would marginally reduce the potential job gain from elimination of the current account deficit.

[3] Department of Economic Research, The Toronto-Dominion Bank, *Business and Economics*, Vol. 8, No. 1 (March 1979), p. 12; Ontario Economic Council, *The Ontario Economy, 1977-1987* (Toronto, 1977), p. 77; Department of Energy, Mines and Resources, *An Energy Strategy for Canada* (Ottawa: Information Canada, 1977).

Chapter 6

[1] Bruce Wilkinson noted some problems concerning Canada's trade: "Canada's surpluses presently exist in those commodities for which the long-run income elasticity of demand is quite low, frequently below unity. In other words, as foreign incomes

expand, the quantity demanded of these products expands less than in proportion to the growth in income. In contrast, our deficits are in those commodities for which the income elasticity of demand is relatively high; that is, as income grows the quantities demanded grow more than in proportion to the income growth." See "Canada's Trade Options." The Ryerson Lectures in Economics, Toronto, February 16, 1978.

[2] It must be recognized that Canadian monetary policy operates in a world financial setting and that this can create difficulties. Not only is Canada located near the vast U.S. financial markets but more recently the development of the Eurodollar financial markets has impinged on Canadian interest rate management by the Bank.

[3] Bank of Canada, *Annual Report of the Governor to the Minister of Finance, 1973*, p. 9.

[4] Department of Finance Press Release, February 27, 1975.

[5] This was done in 1970, causing the federal government some difficulty in financing its requirements at home. In order to purchase those U.S. dollars and place them in its exchange reserves, the federal government had to borrow an equivalent amount in Canadian dollars. It is possible for such financing to be carried out in a non-inflationary manner.

[6] The federal authorities have always argued that they cannot purchase provincial government securities, although the Bank of Canada Act allows them to do so, because they would be showing favouritism to one province or another. The foregoing shows that when they carry out offsetting measures they already show such favouritism and indeed pay subsidies indirectly to those provinces that borrow abroad.

[7] The investment decision can be both adversely or positively affected by the expected future value of the exchange rate. If the exchange rate is expected to fall then imported investment goods will be relatively cheap and sales of future output will reflect a relatively low cost of production. If the exchange rate is expected to rise there is an incentive to delay capital investment in a country that largely imports its capital goods.

[8] Richard G. Lipsey, "The Canadian Dollar: Problems and Prospects." The Ryerson Lectures in Economics, Toronto, January 16, 1978.

[9] Many items in the Canadian balance of payments are highly integrated with the Canadian economy. We are using "exogenous" in this context to indicate a weak link to Canadian economic activity.

[10] In most years there would be sufficient provincial, municipal, and corporate borrowings come due in international markets that actual repurchase would be unnecessary. Thus a substantial current account surplus would provide the funds for the redemption of provincial and other issues coming due over the next decade or more.

[11] "In 1971 provinces, municipalities and business corporations raised a total of $3.5 billion by net new issues of bonds in the market. Of this amount only $0.4 billion was in the form of foreign currency issues. Two years earlier when net new bond issues of these borrowers totalled $2.1 billion, the net issue of foreign currency bonds was $1.4 billion. Thus the sales of Canadian dollar issues rose from $0.7 billion in 1969 to $3.1 billion in 1971." See Bank of Canada, *Annual Report of the Governor to the Minister of Finance, 1971*, p. 7.

Chapter 7

[1] The 1975-78 anti-inflation strategy that successfully moderated wage and salary payments was offset by the inflationary effect of poor productivity and weak business investment.

Appendix B

[1] "The FOMC in 1974: Monetary Policy During Economic Uncertainty," Federal Reserve Bank of St. Louis, *Review*, Vol. 57, No. 4 (April 1975), p. 4.

[2] "The FOMC in 1975: Announcing Monetary Targets," Federal Reserve Bank of St. Louis, *Review*, Vol. 58, No. 3 (March 1976), pp. 9, 10.

[3] "The Federal Open Market Committee in 1977," Federal Reserve Bank of St. Louis, *Review*, Vol. 60, No. 3 (March 1978), p. 11.

[4] "Record of Policy Actions of the Federal Open Market Committee, Meeting Held on May 16, 1978," *Federal Reserve Bulletin* (July 1978), p. 563.

[5] *Ibid*, p. 565.

[6] Paul A. Volcker, "A Broader Role for Monetary Targets," Federal Reserve Bank of New York, *Quarterly Review*, Vol. 2 (Spring 1977), p. 25.